YOU CAN TEACH YOURSELF FLATPICKING GUITAR

by Steve Kaufman

YOU WILL LEARN—

HOW TO BUY A GUITAR
THE CARE AND TREATMENT OF YOUR INSTRUMENT
HOW TO HOLD YOUR GUITAR
THE EASY WAY TO FRET A NOTE
HOW TO READ CHORD CHARTS AND PLAY ALL OF THE BASIC CHORDS
THE MAIN CHORDS USED IN THE COMMON BLUEGRASS KEYS
BASIC BLUEGRASS STRUMMING PATTERNS
BASS RUNS AND WALKS

HAMMER-ONS AND PULL-OFFS
23 SING-ALONG SONGS WITH THE WORDS
HOW TO READ TABLATURE
FINDING THE NOTES ON THE GUITAR
PICKING THE LEAD TO 19 SONGS
CROSSPICKING
PRACTICE TECHNIQUES

Audio Contents

1 Tuning the Guitar (:50)
2 Time Signatures (:32)
3 Buffalo Gals (1:07)
4 Waltz Time "Down in the Valley" (1:57)
5 Aunt Rhody-Key of G & C (1:07)
6 Aunt Rhody-Key of D & A (:41)
7 Standard Strumming Patterns (1:21)
8 More Strumming Patterns (1:04)
9 More Strumming Patterns (1:49)
10 Go Tell It on the Mountain (1:12)
11 Old Joe Clark (:56)
12 Amazing Grace (1:22)
13 In the Pines (1:24)
14 House of the Rising Sun (1:21)
15 Understanding the Tablature (2:01)
16 Eighth Notes-Slides Etc./Page 26 (2:24)
17 Wabash Cannonball (:55)
18 Careless Love (:48)
19 Beautiful Brown Eyes (1:15)
20 Two Dollar Bill (1:25)

21 The Wreck of the Old '97 (1:26)
22 Cripple Creek (1:33)
23 The Girl I Left Behind Me (:47)
24 Lonesome Road Blues (1:28)
25 Turkey in the Straw (:47)
26 Red Haired Boy (1:35)
27 Freight Train (1:16)
28 My Home's Across the Blueridge Mountains (1:13)
29 My Walkin Cane (1:20)
30 Mama Don't Allow No (1:42)
31 Jenny Linde Polka (1:21)
32 Jenny Linde Polka-Faster (:47)
33 Mama Don't Allow No (:48)
34 Mama Don't Allow No-Faster (:26)
35 Freight Train with Hammer Ons (1:18)
36 Freight Train with Pull Offs & Runs (1:14)
37 Way-Faring Stranger (1:20)
38 Wayfaring Stranger-Faster (:58)
39 Homes Across the Blueridge Mountains (1:11)
40 Blueridge Mountains-Crosspicking (:58)

41 Blueridge Mountains-Faster (:30)
42 Turkey in the Straw (1:24)
43 Turkey in the Straw-Faster (:45)
44 Wreck of the Old '97 (1:14)
45 Home Sweet Home (1:18)
46 Home Sweet Home-Faster (:48)
47 Cripple Creek (1:10)
48 The Girl I Left Behind (2:01)
49 Home Sweet Home-Crosspicking (2:02)
50 Red Haired Boy (1:57)
51 Arkansas Traveler/Page 70 (1:32)
52 Arkansas Traveler-Faster (:43)
53 Arkansas Traveler/Page 71 (1:26)
54 Arkansas Traveler-Faster (:43)
55 Cripple Creek (:47)
56 Cripple Creek-Faster (:28)
57 Turkey in the Straw (1:12)
58 Turkey in the Straw-Faster (:48)
59 Mama Don't Allow No/Page 78 (:45)
60 Mama Don't Allow No-Faster (:28)

Online Audio & Video

Audio
www.melbay.com/95190EB
Video
dv.melbay.com/95190
You Tube
www.melbay.com/95190V

MEL BAY

Visit us on the Web at http://www.melbay.com — E-mail us at email@melbay.com

1 2 3 4 5 6 7 8 9 0

Contents

(T) denotes On (T)ape

About the Author

Steven S. Kaufman was born on April 20, 1957, in New York City. He was introduced to music at an early age. His father was a jazz pianist, his mother a classically trained pianist. At the age of 4, Steve was encouraged to play the piano, and later moved on to the cello. At 10 he started playing the guitar, but after a few years of strumming, put the guitar under the bed. It wasn't until the age of 14 that Steve started "picking" the guitar and he has not put it down since.

Steve Kaufman is the only three-time winner of the prestigious National Flatpicking Championships held in Winfield, Kansas. His music covers a broad range of styles including bluegrass favorites, popular swing standards, Irish and Appalachian fiddle tunes, folk and country classics, and novelty tunes. Steve has been pleasing crowds from California to Austria since 1976, performing a wide variety of acts from educational shows in elementary schools through colleges, to major bluegrass festivals and concerts.

Steve keeps busy with his instructional books for Mel Bay Publications, audio and video instructional material for Homespun Tapes, his extensive recording career, his performance and workshop touring agenda, and his Maryville private student schedule.

Some of Steve's instructional titles are *Championship Flatpicking, The Complete Flatpicking Book, Flatpicking The Gospels, Power Flatpicking, Bluegrass Guitar Solos That Every Parking Lot Picker Should Know*—Volumes 1,2 and 3, *Learning To Flatpick* (video), *Steve Kaufman's 2-Hour Bluegrass Work Out*—Volume's One and Two, *A Course In Bluegrass Rhythm* (video), *Intermediate Flatpicking* (Video) and *Easy Gospel Guitar* (Video). More titles will becoming out soon.

Getting Started

The essential items you will need to teach yourself to flatpick are: a) the guitar and b) the flatpick. Let's look at the different options that we have with the guitars. Flatpicking is almost always played on a steel-string acoustic guitar as opposed to a nylon-stringed classical guitar. There are many different styles of acoustic guitars. Martin guitars seemed to have set the standards in the early '30's by giving different sized guitars their names. The most common size of guitar is called a Dreadnought or "D" size. This is the size that I use. It is roughly 40.75 inches in total length, 15.5 inches at its widest point and 4 7/8 inches deep. The "000" size (triple 0) is about 1/4 inch narrower at its widest point. The 00 size is 1/2 inch smaller than the "D," and the 0 is about 3/4 inches smaller. Don't let a smaller-sized guitar fool you. The volume and tone can match the bigger guitars.

Let's talk a little more about different kinds of guitars before we pick one out for you. The student-model guitars start around $100. This kind of guitar is probably going to be a 3/4 size guitar. The size is about right for a 6-9 year old to start with. They look dwarfy on the lap of an average adult. They are generally hard to play, but the repairman at the local music store where the guitar was purchased can adjust the string height so that it is easily played. This is called "adjusting the action." You can buy a good full-sized guitar starting around $175. By good I mean it is the full size, and the longer you play this guitar, the more you will notice the need for something better. These kinds of guitars are laminated wood guitars. This means that the wood may look great on the outside, but inside they may be something completely different. They are like a plywood guitar—mahogany or rosewood for the back and sides, and spruce for the top that are layered together and glued.

Something a little better would be in the $350 to $700 range. This guitar would be constructed of a least a solid top, maybe with a pick-up inside and laminated back and sides. These are good-sounding guitars. The main reason for going for a solid-top guitar is that the more years the instrument is played, the better it will sound. A laminated guitar may sound fine when you purchase it, but it will never sound any better. A completely solid wood guitar will sound richer and fuller as the years roll by (if it is played—they won't sound better by themselves).

The most common woods for a solid-wood guitar are as follows. The neck is usually made of either mahogany or rock maple. The fingerboard is either maple, rosewood or ebony. There are many different woods that are used for the bodies. The most common woods are rosewood, mahogany, koa and maple. The tops are usually made of spruce and sometimes cedar.

My Taylor 810- custom cutaway is made of a mahogany neck, ebony fingerboard, Engleman spruce top and East Indian rosewood back and sides. My Martin has Brazilian rosewood back and sides, silver spruce for the top, mahogany neck and an ebony fingerboard. My Gallagher 72 Special 6-string and custom 7-string guitars are made of East Indian Rosewood back and sides, mahogany neck, ebony fingerboard and a sitka spruce top. All of my guitars have a wide fingerboard measuring 1 3/4" at the nut. My 7-string Gallagher guitar measures 2 1/8" at the nut.

Some of My Guitars

Taylor 810 Custom

1934 Reissue Martin
D-28 Herringbone

1978 Gallagher 72-Special

1992 Gallagher 72-Special
Cut-a-way 7-string

Buying a Guitar

What to look for when you are investing in a guitar? The first question is price. Do not spend more than you can afford, but buy the best guitar that you can afford. If a good guitar is selling for $300 and you have $400 to spend, but a far better guitar is hanging on the wall for $500, then do one of three things. First, ask if they'll take $400 for the better one. Second, ask if you can buy the $300 guitar and trade back later—getting your whole investment towards the next better guitar. Or thirdly, wait the amount of time it takes to get the money together for the better guitar. I teach in a music store and this is the same advice I give my students. These are the three steps in buying the best guitar that you can afford.

Now you have your eye on a guitar in the store. Check the warranty. Will the store service the instrument if it needs work later? Look at all of the glue joints. This is any place where two pieces of wood are joined. The neck to the body. The top to the sides. The sides to the back. The bridge to the top. You should not be able to see a gap or any kind of air space at any of these joints. Look down the fingerboard. It should not be overly bowed or warped. Guitar fingerboards will have a slight bow in them, but we are talking about only .11 to .17 of an inch. If you didn't know what to look for, you wouldn't notice this amount of a bow. If you see any kind of warping or any body seams coming unglued, then put the guitar back. If the store says they can fix it, have them fix it first and guarantee it.

You now have a good guitar in your possession. Next you'll need some flatpicks. I use the Tortex medium gauge, standard Fender-style picks. I like this gauge because they have the right amount of resistance and a clear treble tone. I hit the strings pretty hard, so I can't use the regular plastic picks. They (cellulos picks) tend to break for me after about one half hour of picking. Nylon picks and real thick picks will absorb some of the highs (treble). Try to stay with at least a medium gauge for flatpicking. Find a shape or style of pick and stay with it for a while. Try not to jump around to different size or gauge picks. This will only confuse your right hand.

You'll also need a capo. Around here they are called either a hillbilly crutch or a cheater. I will be calling them any of these three names and going into their use later in this manual. I use the Shubb capo, but in case you don't want to spend around $20 for a capo, the double elastic kind will work fine. See the capo picture for an idea of the different kinds of capos on the market.

You can go ahead and pick up a strap, though you probably won't be using it in the beginning. If you see a strap that you like—go and get it. Adjust your strap so that whether you are sitting or standing the guitar will be in roughly the same place (see the pictures). I've noticed that Doc Watson wears his strap kind of tight. If he is sitting, you can see that the bottom of his guitar is about an inch up and off of his leg. This way he can tap his foot and not have it effect, or bounce, his guitar.

You may need to get an electronic tuner. They range in price from $30 up to several hundred dollars. I use the Sabine ST-1500 tuner. I like it because it is a chromatic tuner. This means that it can tune any note as opposed to some of the lower priced guitar tuners that only tune the six open strings: E,B,G,D,A and E. A chromatic tuner will get you in tune if you have a capo on any fret because it can tell you if any note is in tune. My tuner does not have a needle to tell me if I'm in tune. It uses blinking LED lights. If you are a beginning tuner I would suggest purchasing a tuner and then wean yourself away from it as you get more accustomed to the way the guitar should sound when it is properly tuned.

There are basically two types of strings on the market. Nylon and steel. Nylon strings are used by classical, and sometimes jazz, players, while steel strings are used by everybody else. I know more about the steel strings, so I'll confine my specialization to this kind of string. I use the Dr. Tite Strings (41 Allen Street, Cresskill, NJ 07626). Tell Mark I sent ya. They are medium gauge, "Rare Phosphor Bronze" strings, starting with a .13 first string to a .56 on the low E bass string. There are several string manufacturers to mention—John Pearse, Martin, GHS, to name a few. Try different strings until you find the best for you and your instrument.

Don't let strings stay on the guitar for more than 8 months. Under normal conditions, the strings will "go dead" somewhere between 1-4 months. You should change them whenever you notice that the new-sounding brilliance is no longer present. As I mentioned earlier, I use medium-gauge strings. I like the volume and tone that are produced only by mediums. Light-gauge strings tend to rattle or buzz if you hit them hard. In hearing the buzzing, you will have a tendency to play softer. In playing softly you will not develop to your fullest, so the options are to use light strings and raise the action or string height up or use medium strings and set the action low enough that the strings don't buzz when you hit them.

The Care and Feeding Of Your Instrument

The three main dangers to any acoustic instrument are heat, cold and humidity. A quick change from any of these conditions can be very dangerous to your guitar. Don't leave the guitar in the trunk all day long on a hot summer's day. Any or all of the glue joints can come unglued. Don't let your instrument get cold in the winter and then bring it inside the house and put it next to the heater with hopes of warming it up quicker. It will warm up quicker but it will also get a lot of finish cracks at the least and wood cracks at the most. If you live in a dry area, you may need to keep a humidifying device in your case. A damp sponge in a soap box works well.

Clean your guitar with any wood polish that doesn't have wax in it. I usually use Lemon Pledge furniture polish or Martin guitar polish. They seem to sound better when there is not a blanket of accumulated grit and dirt on them. They seem happier too. Use some kind of oil on the fingerboard at least once a year. This will prevent drying and cracking of your fingerboard. It is a good idea to use rubbing alcohol on a clean rag to wipe your strings off after you've been playing. It helps to keep the grit and grime out of the windings of your bass strings. Norman Blake taught me a trick to bring life back to your wrapped bass strings. Loosen the tension to near nothing on your bass strings. Pull the string away from the fingerboard and let it go. It will sound like a gun going off but it's really shaking the dirt out of the windings. Loosen only one string at a time for this procedure.

You may also want to purchase a guitar stand. They are all pretty much the same. They keep your guitar out in the open, in plain sight, calling to every time you walk by saying, "Play me, play me." Watch out for little children, brothers, sisters and animals bumping into it or knocking it over.

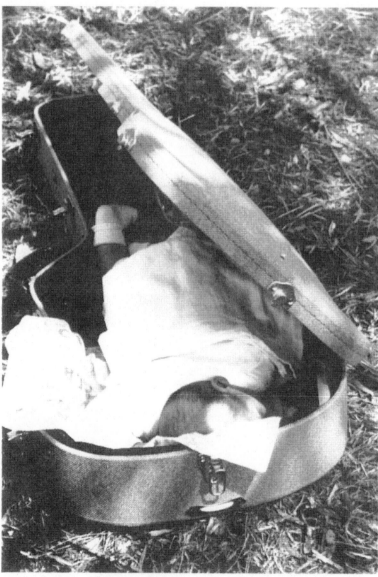

Mark Oliver Dixon Kaufman sleeping in my case while I performed a work-shop at the Merle Watson Memorial Festival, Wilkesboro, N.C., April 1993.

Holding the Guitar

Hold the guitar so that the bottom side is lying flat on your leg (see picture). Do not lean the guitar back in order to see your gingers or the strings. Get used to where strings are by remembering your mistakes. You should try to memorize your music because you want to be able to watch your left hand, and you can't look at two things at once. Do not play the guitar while reclining on the bed or on the couch. Use a straight-back chair that has no arms, something like a kitchen chair. I like to practice in an armless rocking chair.

Left-Hand Position

In order to keep the left hand organized, we will number your left-hand fingers. The pointer or index finger is number one. Your next finger is two, ring finger is three and little finger (pinky) is now the fourth finger. You want to have as little surface area of the hand touching the neck and fingerboard as possible. Keep your thumb pointed up with just the thumbprint area touching the neck. Place your thumbprint on the neck where the 4th and 5th string are on the fingerboard. This should be about 3/4 of the way up the curve of the neck from the bottom to the top (see picture). Use only your fingertips to fret the possible without going over the fret to the next note. This will be the easiest place to fret the note. It will also guarantee not to buzz or rattle. It takes very little pressure to hold a note down with the left hand. If you find yourself pushing hard enough to turn your fingernails white, then you are pushing too hard. Try adjusting your fingers a little towards the next fret. If this doesn't remedy the buzzing, then have your instrument checked out at your local music store for high-string action or a warped neck.

Sitting

Standing Comfortably

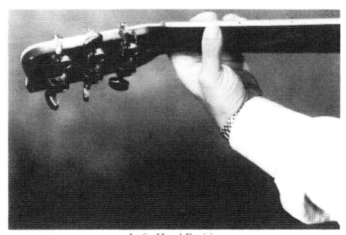

Left -Hand Position

Holding the Pick With the Right Hand

Grip the pick with your index finger and thumb. The thumbprint of your right hand should be right over the name on the pick. Your index finger should squeeze the pick from its outside edge, meaning that *your index fingerprint should not show up on the pick.* Your thumb should be able to bend at the first knuckle. This will allow some more movement and flexibility. Your thumb is your volume control. The tighter you squeeze your thumb—the more resistance you will have as you strum or hit the string(s). With the right amount of follow through and a tight thumb gripping, the pick you will produce more volume that if you held the pick loosely.

The right hand will hold the pick with the thumb and first finger only. Be sure to hold the pick in such a way that your first knuckle of your thumb can bend. This is important to achieve the snappy but loose, crisp tone that will set you apart from other flatpickers. One way to look at your right-hand approach is to look at very good "Texas" fiddlers. They pull the bow from right to left and left to right. These are the equivalent of our down-up swings. Just at the last instant of their pulling the bow, from the elbow, the fiddler gives a final push or pull with the wrist. This gives them a little more drive in their sound.

You can get a lot of drive from your thumb. Your thumb is also your volume switch. The tighter your thumb muscle gets directly relates to the volume that you gain (see picture). Be sure not to tighten your thumb to the extent of locking your wrist. You'll want your wrist to be able to swing freely. I like the way a buddy of mine put the right-hand wrist action. His name is Norman Blake and he's one of the grandest flatpickers of our time. He says that you should make your right-hand action look as if you were shaking off water.

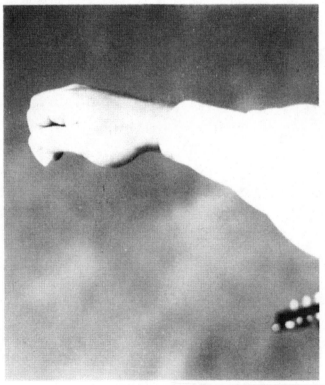

Holding the Pick

Right-Arm Placement

You should let your right arm rest at the elbow on the side of the guitar (see picture). Your arm should be able to swing freely. If you have too much arm hanging over the edge, you will cut off the artery that runs on the underside of the arm, causing your fingers to go numb and fall asleep. Keep the arm right at the elbow joint and you will have plenty of mobility.

Left-Hand Posture

Your left hand should not be in contact with the neck of the guitar other than your thumb pushing on the back of the neck and your fingertips pushing on the strings. Do not hold the guitar neck like a baseball bat. Your thumb should have very little pushing force, and your fingers don't need to push very hard. The less skin that you have on the neck—the less friction you will have when you try to move up or down the neck (see picture).

Right-Hand Placement On the Top of the Guitar

The first picture shows the right hand just about to swing at a string. Notice that the heel of the palm is high and off the bridge. The little finger is making contact with the top of the guitar. The little finger is your depth guide and support.

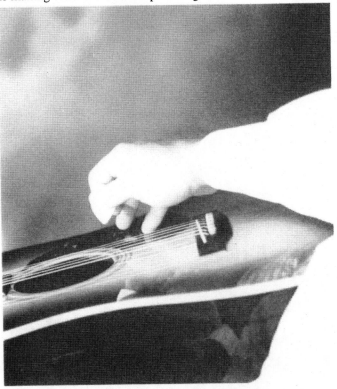

The second picture shows the depth of the strike. Notice that the ring finger is now making slight contact with the top. The ring finger is very loose and will bounce around a little. Don't let your right hand get too tight. The pick is about 3/8-inch into the string with a forward rotation of about 20 degrees. Try not to hit the strings with the flat of the pick. By rotating your pick this way, you will find less resistance of the pick to the strings, therefore allowing you to play a little faster. If you rotate your pick in this manner you will wear out the bottom left edge and the top right edge.

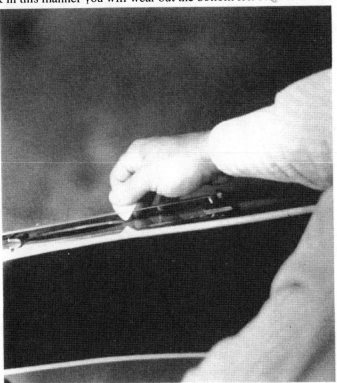

The Easy Way To Fret a Note

The easiest way to fret a note is to push with just the tip of the fingers. Make sure that you are as far in the fret as you can be without going into the next fret (see picture). It doesn't take much pressure to hold a note down, so if you notice yourself holding the note with a death grip, your fingertips turning white and your knuckles hurting, then you are pushing too hard.

Holding and fretting a C chord.
Notice: Fingertips as far in the fret as possible.

Reading the Chord Charts

The chord chart, or chord diagram, is the best way for teachers to give students a visual idea of where to place their fingers on the fingerboard in order to learn the different chords. Hold your guitar out in front of you with the high E string on the right and the low E string on the left. Your strings are vertical and the frets are horizontal. The chord diagrams are written the same way.

How To Read a Chord Diagram

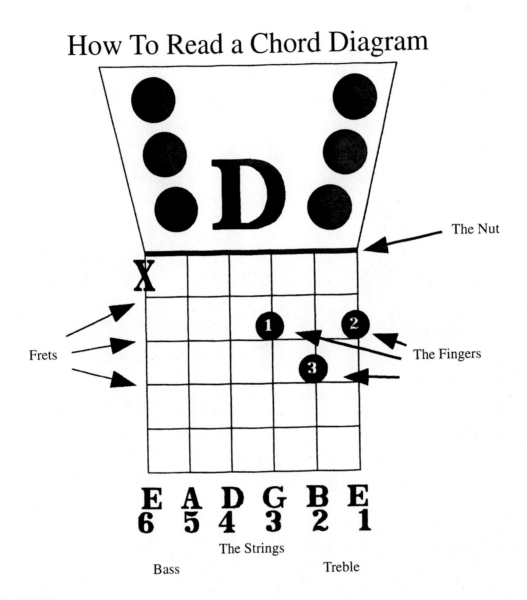

The Nut

X

Frets

① 1 ② 2

③ 3

The Fingers

E A D G B E
6 5 4 3 2 1

The Strings

Bass   Treble

Reading the Chord Diagrams

The **horizontal lines represent the frets**. The **vertical lines represent the strings** as they come down the length of the fingerboard. The **dots** on the fingerboard **represent your fingers** pushing on the frets. Look at the vertical line farthest to the right. This is the first string—high E. The dot on this string is in the second fret. See how it is in the second box or fret from the dark line or the nut? This indicates to you to put your second finger on the first string, second fret. When you put a finger on a string, make sure that your finger is fretting the note as far to the right in the fret as it can go without going into the next higher fret. This is the easiest place to fret a note and it takes the least amount of pressure. Leave this finger down while you find another dot or finger. You do this until all of the dots represented in the graph are found on the guitar fingerboard. Look at the sixth string (farthest to the left). There is an "X" on this string, meaning that it is not to be played or strummed.

Practice holding the chord as it is shown. Release the chord and shake your left hand out and try to get back to the chord as quickly as you can. This is a great way to practice any new chord.

The Main Chords That Are Most Commonly Used For Each Key

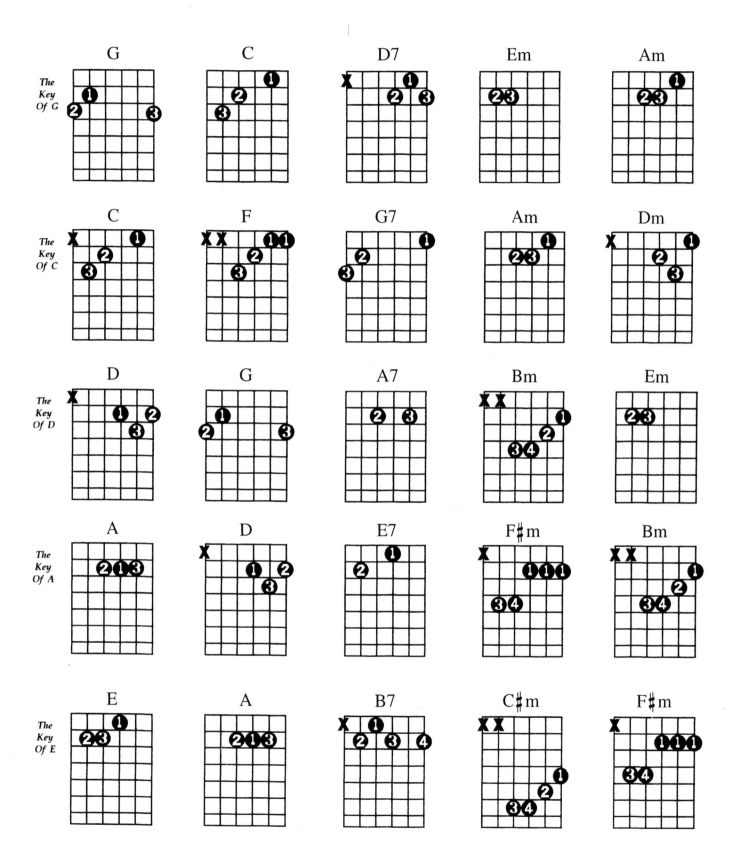

Time Signatures

A diagonal line (/) represents one strum. When strumming, it is customary to **strum with a down swing on the down beat** from the bass strings to the treble strings. You can strum with an **up swing from the treble strings to the bass strings on the up beat.**

$$\frac{4}{4} \text{ or } C = \textbf{COMMON TIME}$$

4/4 time means that you will have four (4) beats in all of the measures, and that each strum, or down swing, will represent one (1) beat. *Be sure to hold the chord that is written over each measure.*

Buffalo Gals

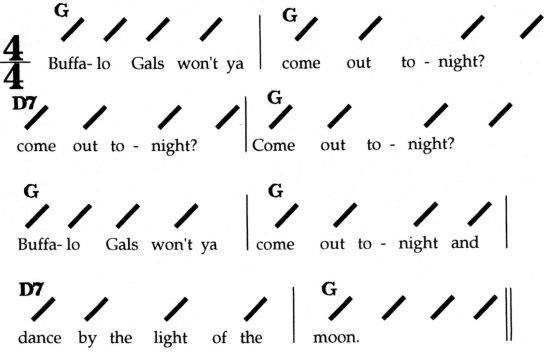

G / / / / | G / / / /
Buffa- lo Gals won't ya | come out to - night?

D7 / / / / | G / / / /
come out to - night? | Come out to - night?

G / / / / | G / / / /
Buffa- lo Gals won't ya | come out to - night and

D7 / / / / | G / / / /
dance by the light of the | moon.

$$\frac{3}{4}$$ = THREE-FOUR or WALTZ TIME

3/4 time means that you will have three (3) beats in all of the measures, and that each strum, or down swing, will represent one (1) beat. Try playing "Down In the Valley" with three strums every measure. *Be sure to hold the chord that is over each measure.*

Down In The Valley

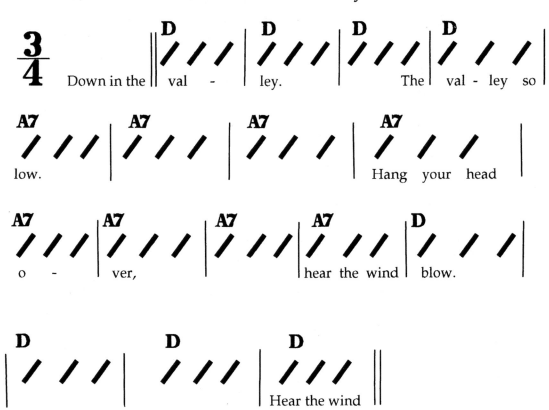

Let's Get Used To the Four Main Keys

What does it mean when we talk about the "key of G?" When someone mentions the key of G to me, I immediately think of the three main chords that I will be strumming. In the key of G, they are G, C and D7. Looking at the chart of **The Main Chords That Are Commonly Used For Each Key,** I can see which chords will be linked together for the different keys. The chart does not tell me what the order of the chords is but it does tell me what chords to think of and a log of chords that I don't have to think of. If I am playing a standard type of bluegrass flatpicking song in the key of C, I will more than likely be using C, F and G7. The key of C will almost definitely (a 90% chance) start and end on C; at some point I will hear the chord change. Either before the change actually occurs or after it is too late, and I'll have to remember the change spot the next time I get through the song. Then I am going to change chord from C to either F or G7. Those are my most common choices and I don't have to think about the hundreds of other chords in all of the chord books. I have a 50/50 chance of hitting the correct chord. Those are good odds anywhere. If it is supposed to go to F and I pick G7, I immediately jump to F upon hearing the unmatched tones of my guitar and I remember the spot where the F is supposed to go for the next time through the song. The next chord change works the same way. You have a 50/50 chance of hitting the right chord.

I've written out "Go Tell Aunt Rhody" in four different keys in order for you to get used to playing the three main chords in the four main keys. The main chords for the keys come right from my chart. The first chord on the left in each column is the root or key chord. The chart is here to help you figure out which chords will fit together and how they are related to each other. If you are playing a song in the key of G but you find you cannot sing it in this key, then you simply **transpose** it to another key. This sounds hard but it is really a simple method, particularly when you have a chart to go by. The chord structure for the imaginary song you are playing is G to D7 to C, back to G, and then it starts over. Look at the chart and find the line for the key of G and you will find these three chords. See how they jump around and are not in the same order as the chart? Now you want to change this to the key of D. Look at the D line and substitute the chords on the D line for the chords on the G line in the same order that you found them before. The G turns into a D, the D7 changes to A7. See what we are doing? The C chord changes to G. All we did was substitute chords from one key with the chords in the same column of another key.

The arrangement of "Aunt Rhody" will get you started strumming. Since we are in 4/4 time (four beats in every measure) we will be strumming four strums in every measure. Each diagonal line is representing one strum. Play through each line over and over until the chord changes smooth out. Each time you go through the line it will get faster. Each time you play a line it will be helping out the next line. Play steady, don't play too soft, and don't rush anything by practicing mistakes. Have fun with it!

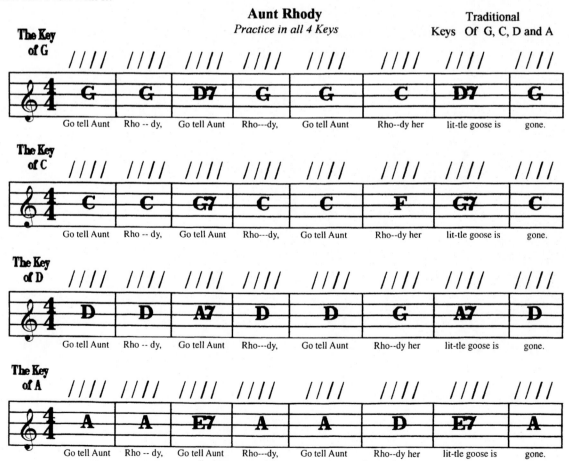

Aunt Rhody
Practice in all 4 Keys

Traditional
Keys Of G, C, D and A

16

The Standard Bluegrass Strumming Patterns for Chords for 4/4 and 3/4 Time

Let's start learning some bluegrass strumming patterns. The first thing we have to know is *how many beats are in each measure.* If you have a song written out, like the ones in this book, you can look at the top left corner of the music to find the number of beats. If there is a 3/4 in the corner, you are being told that there are 3 beats in the measure. If there is a 4/4 in the corner, you will have 4 beats in the measure. Just look at the top number of the fraction. The bottom number has something to with the notes and we'll touch on this later. If you don't have a song written out and you are trying to learn it *by ear* you will have to: 1) start tapping your foot on the beat, 2) listen for the chord changes and 3) start counting the beats that occur in the patterns, or measures, before the pattern repeats itself. The number will probably be a 4 or a 3. This will tell you how many beats there are in each measure. The more you do this, the easier it gets.

Once you have the number of beats established you can see which rhythm pattern you want to use. The easiest one to use its the one-strum-per-beat method. This is what we did in "Aunt Rhody." Next you would use a bass-strum pattern. If you have 3 beats in a measure, you would either strum 3 times or you would hit a bass-strum-strum pattern. Each note and/or strum takes one beat to perform giving you the proper number of beats in 3/4 time. If you are playing in 4/4 time you would either strum 4 times in the measure or you would hit a bass-strum-bass-strum pattern. We will be getting into bass walks in the songs a little later. For right now, let's just get our timing down.

The following measures are not songs. Rather, they are the standard rhythm patterns for most bluegrass chords in both 4/4 and 3/4 time. I did not write out strumming 3 or 4 times for each chord. This was to see if you actually read through these paragraphs. The 3-or-4-strum-per-measure method should be the first way you work out any song if you are a beginner. It's tough changing the chords on time, and I don't feel you need to worry about which bass notes to hit before each strum. Go through the songs with the "1-strum-per-beat" method, and you will be able to change your chords with less trouble. Memorize the bass notes used with each chord. They are standard bass notes for these chords. Keep in mind if you make a mistake, don't stop—unless you keep making the same mistake. If you make the same mistake over and over, then you will have to stop and figure out what you are doing wrong. Go slowly and steadily.

Understanding the Chord Rhythm Charts To Boom-Chuck-Boom-Chuck or Boom-Chuck-Chuck

The **numbers over the measures indicate the strings to hit**. *Hit only one string.* The A-chord measure starts with a "5." This means hit the 5th string alone. There is a diagonal(/) line after the "5." **The "/" represents one strum**. If you are playing in 4/4 time, you should be hitting 4 things in each measure (Bass-Strum-Bass-Strum or boom-chuck-boom-chuck). If you are playing in 3/4 time, you should hit 3 things in each measure (Bass-Strum-Strum or Boom-chuck-chuck). In the beginning we will be hitting a "Bass-Strum-Bass-Strum" pattern. As we go, on we will get into walking the bass notes around a little bit. Learn, practice and memorize the rhythm pattern for each chord. Again, go slowly and steadily.

The Standard Bluegrass Strumming Patterns For Chords In 4/4 Time and 3/4 Time

The A family's strumming pattern in 4/4 time consists of hitting the 5th string then strum. Next hit the 6th string and strum.

The A family's strumming pattern in 3/4 time consists of hitting the 5th string then strum-strum. If there is a second measure of A, you would hit the 6th string then strum-strum. This goes for A, Am or A7.

5 / 6 /	5 / /	6 / /
A	A	A

The B and Bm bar chord strumming pattern in 4/4 time consists of hitting the 5th string then strum. Next hit the 6th string and strum. When playing the B7, you will hit the 5th string and strum. Next move your finger from the 5th string 2nd fret to the 6th string, 2nd fret. Hit the 6th string then strum. *This movement is noted by the circle around the "6" above the B7 measure.*

The B family's strumming pattern in 3/4 time consists of hitting the 5th string then strum-strum. If there is a second measure of B, you would hit the 6th string then strum-strum. The strings hit in the B7 3/4 time pattern are played the same way. *Be sure to move your 5th finger to the 6th string if there are two measures of B7.*

5 / 6 /	5 / ⑥ /	5 / /	⑥ / /
B and Bm bar chords	B7	B7	B7

The C family's chord strumming pattern in 4/4 time consists of hitting the 5th string then strum. Next hit the 6th string and strum. Next move your finger from the 5th string, 3rd fret to the 6th string, 3rd fret. Hit the 6th string then strum. *This movement is noted by the circle around the "6" above the C measure.*

The C family's strumming pattern in 3/4 time consists of hitting the 5th string then strum-strum. If there is a second measure of C, you would move your finger from the 5th string, 3rd fret to the 6th string, 3rd fret and hit the 6th string then strum-strum.

5 / ⑥ /		5 / /	⑥ / /
C		C	C

The D family's strumming pattern in 4/4 time consists of hitting the 4th string then strum. Next hit the 5th string and strum.

The D family's strumming pattern in 3/4 time consists of hitting the 4th string then strum-strum. If there is a second measure of D, you would hit the 5th string then strum-strum. This goes for D, Dm and D7.

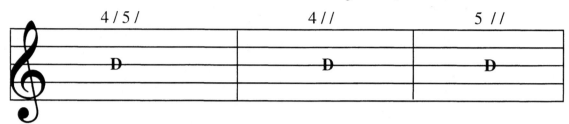

The E family's strumming pattern in 4/4 time consists of hitting the 6th string first then strum. Next hit the 5th or 4th string and strum. This goes for E, Em and E7.

The E family's strumming pattern in 3/4 time consists of hitting the 6th string then strum-strum. If there is a second measure of E, you would hit the 6th or 5th string then strum-strum.

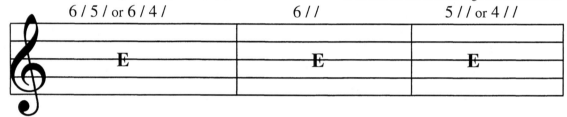

The F family's chord strumming pattern in 4/4 time consists of hitting the 4th string then strum. Next move your finger from the 4th string, 3rd fret to the 5th string, 3rd fret. Hit the 5th string then strum. *This movement is noted by the circle around the "5" above the C measure.*

The F family's strumming pattern in 3/4 time consists of hitting the 4th string then strum-strum. If there is a second measures of F, you would move your finger from the 4th string, 3rd fret to the 5th string, 3rd fret and hit the 5th string then strum-strum.

4 / ⑤ /   4 / /   ⑤ / /

F   F   F

The G family's strumming pattern in 4/4 time consists of hitting the 6th string first then strum. Next hit the 5th or 4th string and strum. *This goes for G, Gm and G7.*

The G family's strumming pattern in 3/4 time consists of hitting the 6th string then strum-strum. If there is a second measure of G, you would hit the 6th or 5th string then strum-strum.

6 / 5 / or 6 / 4 /   6 / /   5 / / or 4 / /

G   G   G

Let's Get Started

We've covered the three main chords that are most often used in each of the most common bluegrass keys. We've learned how to hit the strums and/or the bass-strum pattern depending upon how many beats are in each measure. Now it's time to start playing the rhythm to some songs.

We will start with "Go Tell It On the Mountain." The first thing we have to look for are the number of beats in each measure. Look in the top left corner and you will see a 4/4. Remember that this tells us that we will be dealing with 4 beats in each measure. Now we have to decide if we are going to strum 4 times in each measure, or are we going to use a boom-chuck-boom-chuck pattern. You can do either one as long as you play 4 "things" in each measure. If you have trouble switching the chords quickly, just strum 4 times each measure—slowly.

I've decided to write this tune out using the bass-strum, or boom-chuck method. Notice that all of the D chords start with a 4th-string bass note, then strum, then a 5th-string bass note and strum. All of the A chords use the 5th and 6th strings for the bass notes. Get used to these bass notes with these chords and you won't have to think about which to hit later on. This will make you a faster rhythm player. Be sure to play along with the recording.

Go Tell It On The Mountain

Starting Note

Traditional
Key of D

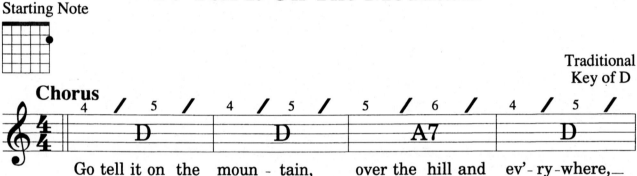
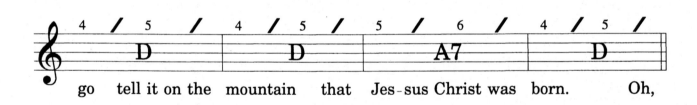
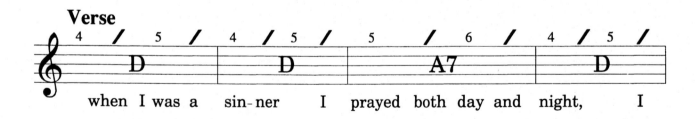
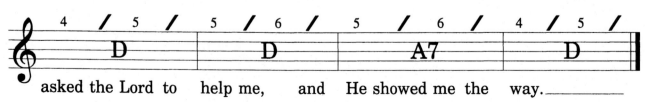

Old Joe Clark

"Old Joe Clark" is a fiddle tune from way back. It's a song about a mean ol' man. Maybe this is the reason it's played so fast. I have written the song out to follow the words. If you are playing this tune as an instrumental, you are to play the first 8 measures (the verse) twice. Then go on to the chorus and play it twice also. But the words just allow for the song to be played with no repeats.

Notice which bass notes are being hit with each chord. Measure 7 of both the verse and the chorus are "split measures." This means that you have two chords in the measure. The measure has 4 beats and both chords have to get equal time. So you need to hit the 5th string and strum the A chord, then switch to the E7 chord and hit the 6th string and strum. This is a very fast change. Practice this chord change about 15 times. Then try to play the entire passage without slowing down at these "split measures."

Starting Note

Traditional
Key of A

Verse

5 / 6 /	5 / 6 /	5 / 6 /	5 / 6 /
A	A	A	E7

I used to live on a moun-tain top. Now I live in town. I'm

5 / 6 /	5 / 6 /	5 / 6 /	5 / 6 /
A	A	A E7	A

stay-ing at the big ho - tel, court-ing Bet - sy Brown.

Chorus

5 / 6 /	5 / 6 /	5 / 6 /	6 / 4 /
A	A	A	G or E7*

Fare ye well, Old Joe Clark, Fare ye well I'm bound,

5 / 6 /	5 / 6 /	5 / 6 /	5 / 6 /
A	A	A E7	A

Fare ye well, Old Joe Clark, good- bye Bet - sy Brown.

* This measure indicates that either a G chord or an E7 will work. The original old-time version of "Old Joe Clark" used an E7. Most of today's pickers, myself included, use a G. I remember jamming with John Hartford one day. We were picking "Old Joe Clark." John was playing fiddle with me on guitar. I picked through the first part and when I got to the second part and used "that G chord" John jumped up and shouted "I hate that chord there. It wasn't written that way!" Ever since then, if I'm playing with someone new, I get a little quieter when it comes time for the G measure. There are many tunes that have been changed and adapted over the years. The only way you find out is to play with as many people as you can. Get out there—it's fun.

John Hardy

Traditional
Key of G

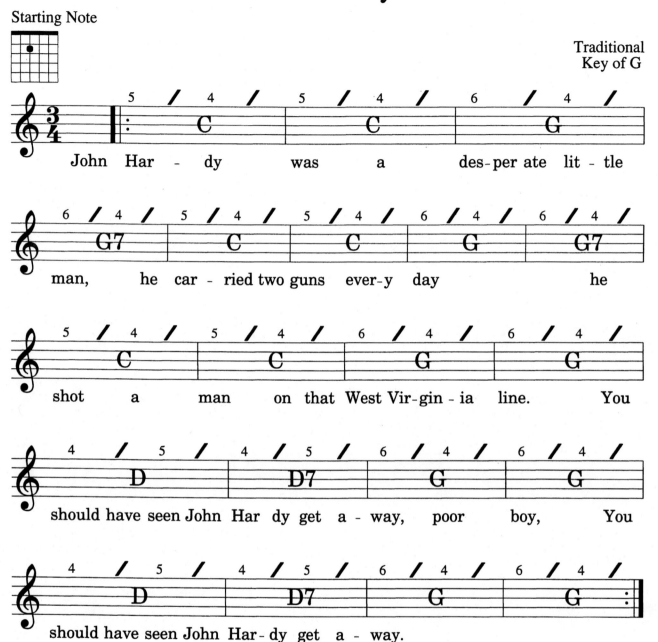

2. He went across to the East Stone Bridge.
There he thought he'd be free.
Up steps the sheriff and he takes him by the arm
saying "Johnny come along with me, poor boy,
Johnny come along withe me".

3. He sent for his mama and his papa too
to come and go his bail.
But there weren't no bail on a murder charge.
so they threw John Henry in jail, poor boy,
threw John Henry in jail.

4. John Hardy had a pretty little girl.
The dress she wore was blue.
She came into the jailhouse hall
saying "Johnny I'll be true to you, poor boy,
Johnny I'll be true to you".

Amazing Grace

"Amazing Grace" is our first 3/4 time song. Be sure that you play a steady three beats per measure. You may want to strum the chords three times each measure the first couple of passes through this one. This will help to keep your tempo steady. Do you remember what a G7 chord will more than likely lead into? What about the D7? Here is a typical example of standard chord changes. This is also not directly related to bluegrass but to nearly all musical styles.

We are also introducing the Em and the Am into the picture. When you hold an Em chord, you should use your 2nd finger on the 5th string and the 3rd finger on the 4th string. By doing this you can easily switch to Am by dropping your 2nd and 3rd fingers down to the 4th and 3rd strings and be able to keep them in the same position. Then all you will have to do is add in the 1st finger on the 2nd string. Keep it steady and notice which strings you are using for the bass notes for each chord.

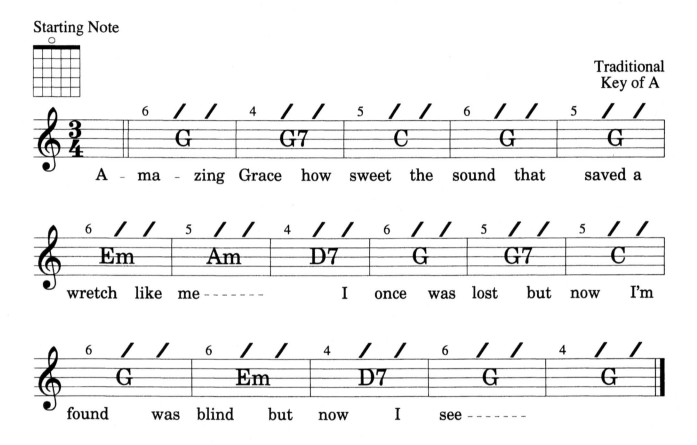

2. T'was grace that taught my heart to fear;
   And grace my fears relieved;
   How precious did that grace appear;
   The hour I first believed.

3. Through many dangers, toils and snares
   I have already come;
   His grace has brought me safe this far
   And grace will lead me home.

4. When we've been there ten thousand years,
   Bright shining as the sun,
   We've no less days to sing God's praise
   Than when we first began.

23

In The Pines

"In the Pines" will be our first piece in the key of C. We will be working on two chords that are somewhat difficult—the C7 and the F chord. The best way to look at and hold down the C7 chord is to hold a regular C chord and then add your little finger on the 3rd string. It will comfortably go to the third string, so this shouldn't be much of a strain. The F chord on the other hand is one of the most difficult chords that you will have to learn. It's not hard to hold when you get used to it, but in the beginning it is difficult to hold down 2 strings with one finger. The best way I can describe holding down the 1st and 2nd string with your first finger is to hold down the F chord as the diagram on the chord page shows. With the left hand in place, but with no pressure on the F chord, pull your left elbow to your side. This action rolls your left-hand first finger on its side. Now it's time to push down on the fingerboard. It doesn't take too much time to push down on the fingerboard. It doesn't take too much down pressure to sound out an F chord, you just have to hold it just right. If you can't get any sound out of an F chord the first couple of times you try, don't worry. Move your fingers just a little bit or release the chord and replace it. You will eventually get a crystal-clear F chord.

Be sure to alternate your ring finger on the left hand from the 5th string to the 6th string for your bass notes. "In the Pines" is a very slow song, so take your time and have fun with it.

Starting Note

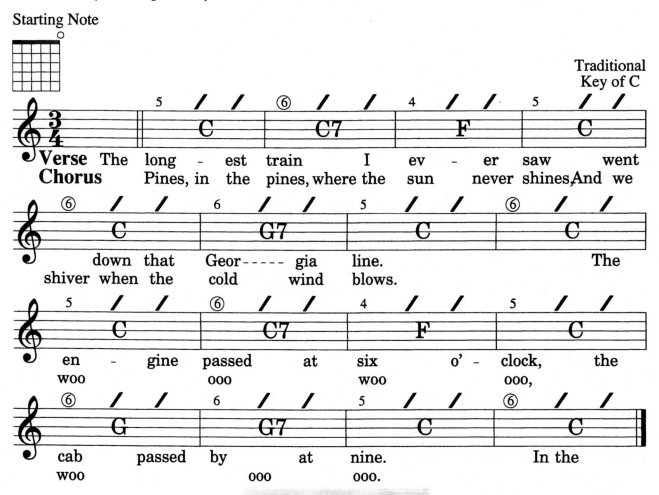

2. I asked my captain for the
   time of day, he said he'd
   thrown his watch a - way.
   It's along steel rail and a
   short cross tie I'm
   on my way back home.

   Chorus

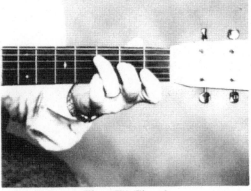

The "F" Chord

3. Little girl, little girl, what
   have I done to
   make you treat me so?
   You've caused me to weep,
   you've caused me to mourn
   you've caused me to leave my home.

   Chorus

24

House Of The Rising Sun

"The House of the Rising Sun" is one of the first tunes that I teach my private students once they learn their first few chords and particularly the F chord.

The first chord change is from Am to C. If you are holding the Am correctly, this will be an easy change. All you have to do is pivot your third finger from the 3rd string to the 5th string. Leave your 1st and 2nd finger down, because there is no need to lift them off the strings to change from Am to C. This will speed up this chord change. E to E7 is easy enough and E7 to Am is relatively easy. Just drop your first and second fingers down one string each and add your third finger on the 3rd string to complete the Am chord.

This tune should prove a challenge to you. Be sure to play through it using the repeat signs 4 times, and then on the 5th pass through this song skip over the 1,2,3,4 ending and go on to the 5th ending. Go slowly through this one. Practice this tune at least 50 times. It will take that many times to play through it smoothly.

Starting Note

Traditional
Key of Am/ C

There is a house in New Or - leans, they
Moth - er She's a tailor,

call the Ris - ing Sun. It's
sews those new blue jeans.

been the ruin of man - y poor girls, and
hus - band he's a gamb - ling man, way

1.2.3.4. **5.**

Lord I know I'm one My
down in New Or - leans.

3. Go tell my baby sister
   Not to do the thongs I've done,
   Shun that house in New Orleans
   They call the Rising Sun.

4. Go tell my baby sister
   The other's on the trainster
   I'm going back to New Orleans
   To wear that ball and chain.

5. Going back to New Orleans
   My race is nearly run
   I'm going to spend the rest of my life
   Beneath that Rising Sun.

Understanding The Tablature

Tablature is like a paint-by-number system. The numbers represent the frets that you need to hold down, and the horizontal lines represent the strings. The top line represents the first string or the high E. The lowest horizontal line represents the low or bass E string. There are stems attached to each note (number). They represent the speed or timing of each note. The stems also tell you whether the note is a down swing or an up swing. If the note has a stem that is not tied or attached to another note, it will be a down swing. If the note is attached to another note at the bottom (called beamed together), the first note is a down swing and the next note is an up swing.

Quarter Notes
They get one beat each and are hit with a down swing.

Half Notes
They get two beats each and they are hit with a down swing Hit the first note and leave it ringing the amount of time that it would take to hit the next note. Hit the half note one time only.

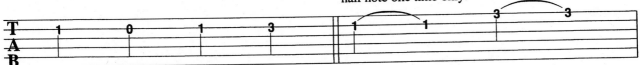

Dotted Half Notes
They get three beats each and they are hit with a down swing. Hit the first note and leave it ringing the amount of time that it would take to hit the next two notes.
Hit the dotted half note one time.

Whole Notes
Whole notes get four beats each. Hit the first note and leave it ringing the amount of time that it would take to hit the note three more times.
Hit the whole note one time only.

Eighth Notes
Eighth notes get half of a beat each. They are grouped together either by two's or four's. The first note is hit with a down swing and the next is hit with an up swing. 2 eighth notes take the same amount of time to hit as one quarter note. Be sure to hit the 1st one down the up-down-up etc.

Slides
A slide is played by hitting the first note, leave the pressure down and slide your finger to the second note. Only hit the first note. When you slide correctly you will hear the second note as loudly as the first. If there is one note written for the slide, you are to start the slide one fret before the notes and stop the slide at the note that is written.

The Hammer On
Hit the first note that is written. Next, let your left hand finger attack the fretboard making contact on the fret with is written for the hammer on. Remember, hit only the first note. The sharper the attack with the left hand -the louder the hammer on will be.

Pull Off
The pull off is the opposite of the hammer on. In this case you will hit the first fretted note and dig your finger under the string and pull it off to the next note. The pull off can only be performed from a higher note to a lower note. The pull off doe not necessarily have to be from a fretted note to an open string. It can be from one fretted note to another fretted note.

Wabash Cannonball

At this point I want to switch us from a standard bass-strum method to the more bluegrass-type boom-chuckin'-bass walkin' style. The easiest way I could teach this style is to use the tablature method. The more that you read the tablature, the easier and faster it gets.

Measures 3 and 11 are standard G-to-C bass walks. They can be used in any rhythm measure of 4/4 time where a G chord directly precedes a C chord. Be sure to hit the bass notes with the same tempo as you hit the bass strum. Many people have a tendency to speed up the bass-walk measures. Be careful.

Measures 4 and 12 are C-walk measures into a D chord.
Measures 7 and 15 are the D-back-to-G walking measures, and measure 16 is a G-to-G measure.

Use these measures in other songs that have the same time signature and chord structure.
The more you use them, the easier they get.

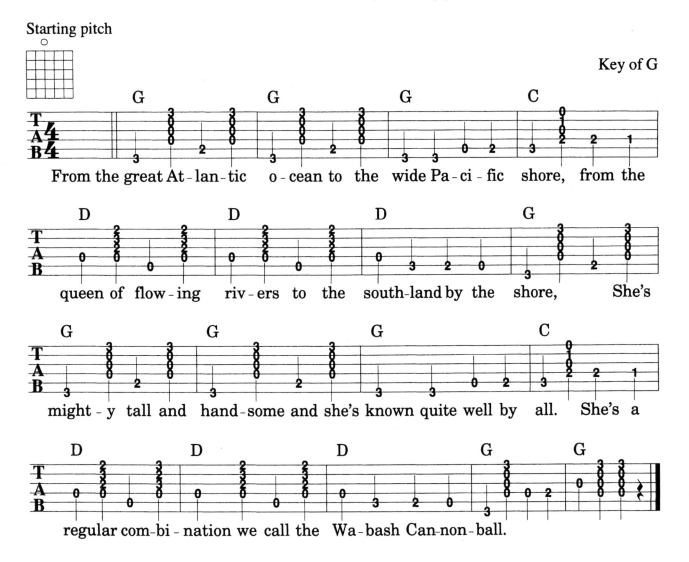

27

Careless Love

"Careless love" consists of different types of bass runs. First of all, it's in the key of D. This opens up some new walks. The first walk is a D to A7. Measure 6 is another example of a D-to-A walk.

Measures 2, 8 and 14 are A7-back-to-D walks.
Measure 10 is a D-to-G walk. It says that you are to play a D7, but it works for D just the same.
Measure 12 is a G-to-D walk-in.

These, like the other walks, will work from a major or 7th chord to a major or 7th chord. It doesn't matter. Take it slow and keep it steady!

Starting pitch

Traditional
Key of D

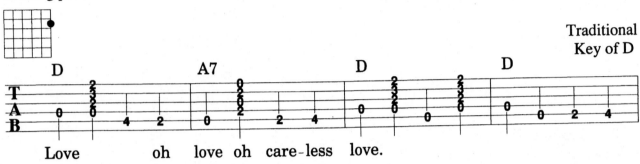

Love   oh   love oh care-less love.

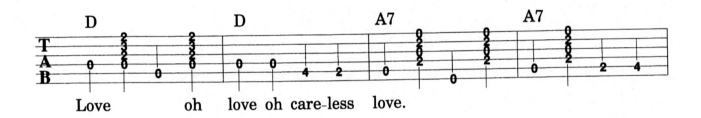

Love   oh   love oh care-less   love.

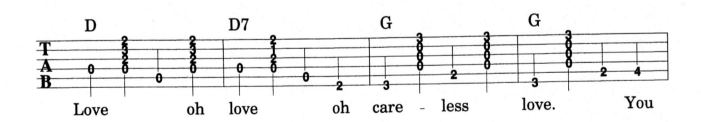

Love   oh   love   oh   care - less   love.   You

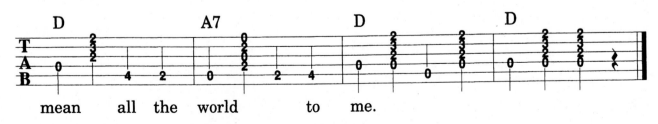

mean   all   the   world   to   me.

Beautiful Brown Eyes

I don't need to say too much about the next three tunes. "Beautiful Brown Eyes" is in 3/4 time. Compare the 3/4 time bass walks to their 4/4 counterparts. See if you can figure out what needed to be taken out of the 4/4 bass-walk measure in order to make them 3/4 bass-walk measures.

Starting pitch

Traditional
Key of C

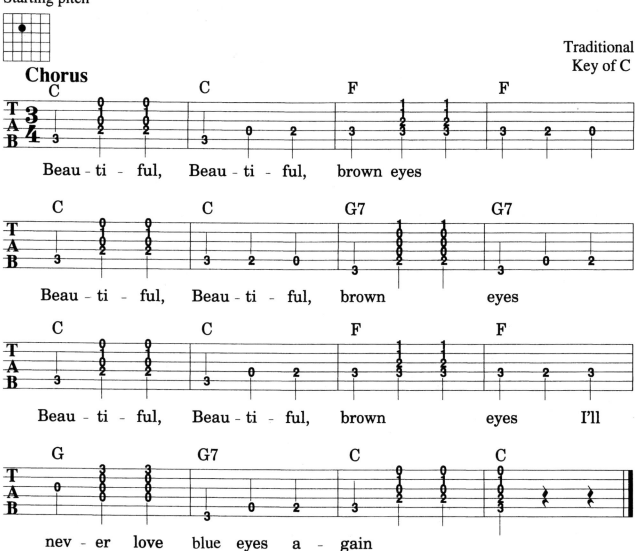

Beau - ti - ful, Beau - ti - ful, brown eyes

Beau - ti - ful, Beau - ti - ful, brown eyes

Beau - ti - ful, Beau - ti - ful, brown eyes I'll

nev - er love blue eyes a - gain

The Verse

1. Willie, my darling I love you,
   Love you with all of my heart;
   Tomorrow we were to be married,
   But liquor has kept us apart.

Chorus

2. I staggered into the barroom,
   I fell down on the floor,
   And the very last words that I uttered,
   "I'll never get drunk any more."

Chorus

3. Seven long years I've been married,
   I wish I was single again.
   A woman don't know half her troubles
   Until she has married a man.

29

Two Dollar Bill

Traditional
Key of A

Starting Pitch

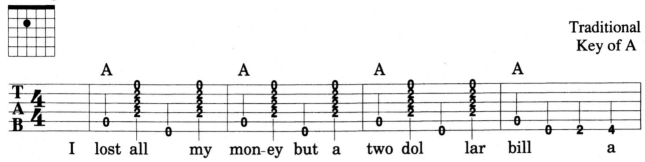

I lost all my mon-ey but a two dol lar bill a

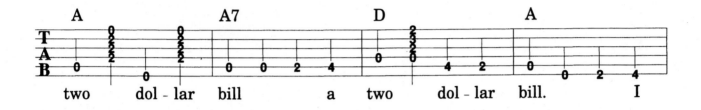

two dol - lar bill a two dol - lar bill. I

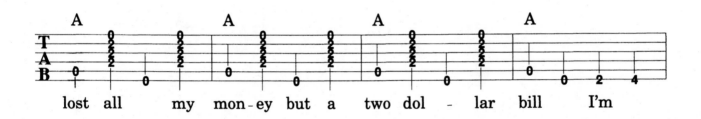

lost all my mon-ey but a two dol - lar bill I'm

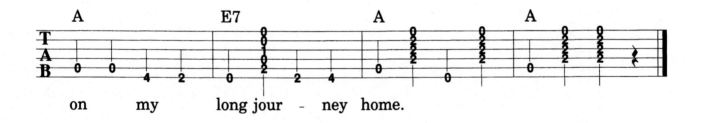

on my long jour - ney home.

2. Black smoke's a-rising and it surely is a train.
   Surely is a train, boys, surely is a train.
   Black smoke's a-rising and it surely is a train.
   I'm on my long journey home.
   Chorus

3. I want to see my woman, I want to see her bad.
   Want to see her bad, boys, I want to see her bad.
   I want to see my woman, I want to see her bad.
   I'm on my long journey home.
   Chorus

The Wreck Of The Old '97

Starting Pitch

Traditional
In The Key of C

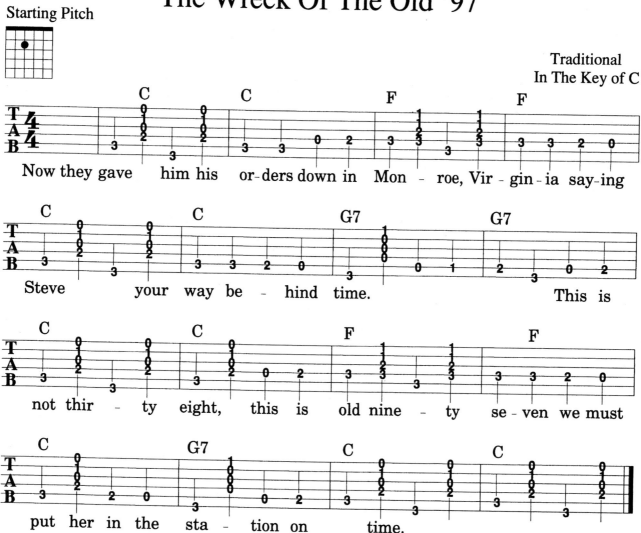

Now they gave him his or-ders down in Mon - roe, Vir - gin - ia say-ing

Steve your way be - hind time. This is

not thir - ty eight, this is old nine - ty se - ven we must

put her in the sta - tion on time.

2. Well he turned and he said to his
tired, greasy fireman.
"Shovel on a little more coal."
And when we cross that White Oak mountain
you can watch old Ninety Seven roll.

3. Well it's a mighty rough road from
Lynchburg to Danville, a line on a three mile grade.
It was on this grade that he lost his leverage,
you can see what a jump he made.

4. He was going down the grade making ninety miles an hour
when his broke whistle broke into a scream.
They found him in the wreck with his hand on the throttle.
Scalded to death by the stream.

5. Now lady's, well, you must take warning
from this time now and learn;
Never speak harsh words to your true, loving husband.
He may leave you and never return.

Cripple Creek

"Cripple Creek" is traditionally a banjo tune. It makes a great Texas-style fiddle tune, which therefore translates to a perfect tune for the flat-top guitar. "Cripple Creek" is a two-part tune. The first part is 4 measures and it is played through twice. The second part, or the chorus, is just the same. I've written this out "straight through," meaning that you start at the beginning and play until the end. You do the same for each verse and chorus. Playing all the way through means picking the verse and chorus 3 times.

Be careful of the split measures in measures 2, 4, 8, 12 and 16. This tune is played very quickly. If you want something to go by, you will start then finish one time through in about 15 seconds. If you can do this, then you will have no need to play faster with anyone—you've achieved full speed.

Have fun with it!

Starting Pitch

2. Girls on Cripple Creek 'bout half grown.
 Jump on a boy like a dog on a bone.
 Roll my britches up to my knees,
 I'll wade old Cripple Creek when I please.
 Chorus

3. Cripple Creek's cold and Cripple Creek's steep,
 I'll wade old Cripple Creek 'fore I sleep.
 Roads are rocky and the hillsides muddy
 and I'm so drunk that I can't stand steady.
 Chorus

32

The Girl I Left Behind Me

The format of this tune is the same as "Cripple Creek." The verse and the chorus are both 4 measures long with repeats. Because we have the lyrics under the measures, I wrote the song straight through. This is another song that is played very quickly, but don't push anything. Speed will always come to you. Just give it enough time to find you.

Starting Pitch

Traditional
Key of G

Verse

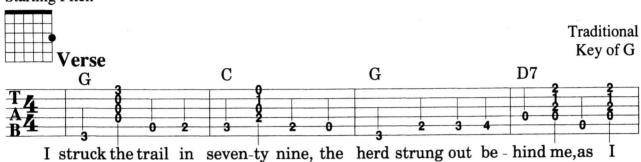

I struck the trail in seven-ty nine, the herd strung out be-hind me, as I

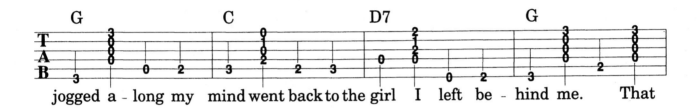

jogged a-long my mind went back to the girl I left be-hind me. That

Chorus

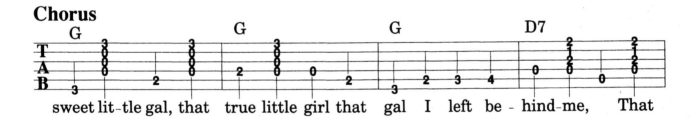

sweet lit-tle gal, that true little girl that gal I left be-hind-me, That

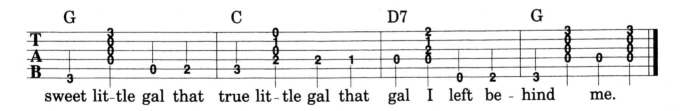

sweet lit-tle gal that true lit-tle gal that gal I left be-hind me.

2. If I ever get off the trail
   And the Indians they don't find me,
   I'll make my way straight back again
   to the girl I left behind me.
   Chorus

3. The wind did blow, the rain did flow,
   the hail did fall and blind me;
   I thought of that gal, that sweet little gal,
   The gal I left behind me.
   Chorus

5. She rode ahead to the place I said,
   I was always glad to find it;
   She says, "I'm true, when you get through,
   Ride back and you will find me.
   Chorus

6. When we sold out, I took the train,
   I knew when I would find her;
   When I got back, we had a smack,
   and that was no gol-darned liar.

Let's Work On Hammer-Ons and Pull-Offs

"Lonesome Road Blues," "Turkey In the Straw," and "Red Haired Boy" are all tunes that I have arranged with hammer-ons. "Lonesome Road Blues" is loaded with bass-walk runs, and in the second to the last measure you will find a pull-off. In this case, it is used as a G-to-G run. It is the beginning to the Lester Flatt G run discussed in the pages that follow. The easiest way to play this run is to use the finger that holds the G chord; 5th string—2nd fret to move over to the 4th string—2nd fret after you hit the strum. Be sure to fret the 2nd fret and then dig your finger under the string and pull it off. This song goes pretty quickly, so get your time in and keep up at the jam sessions.

"Turkey In the Straw" makes use of hammer-ons in the G chord. Use the same finger that holds the 2nd fret on the 5th string while in the G chord. It is the same finger that performed the pull-off in "Lonesome Road Blues." Make sure that when you play the hammer-on that you use the tip of your finger. You must attack the string with the finger of the left hand and keep the pressure down, or the note will sound like a thud.

This arrangement keeps you moving all the time. I'm sure you will find it both enjoyable and challenging.

"Red Haired Boy" has been included in this section because of the hammer-ons but also because of the quick "split measures" between the G and C chords as in measures 2, 6 and 15. Measures 8 and 16 are also quick "splits."

Be sure to play each part twice, and don't slow down for the F chords.

Here I am trying out my new Gallagher 7-string guitar with the maker, Don Gallagher, looking on.
Thanks Don!

Lonesome Road Blues

Traditional
Key of G

Starting Pitch

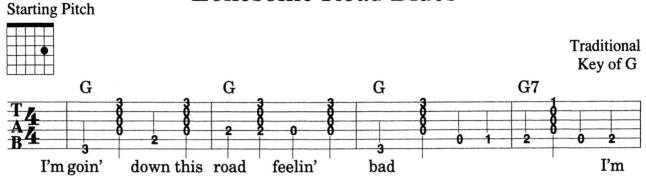

I'm goin' down this road feelin' bad I'm

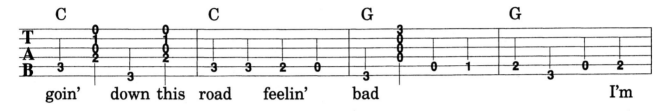

goin' down this road feelin' bad I'm

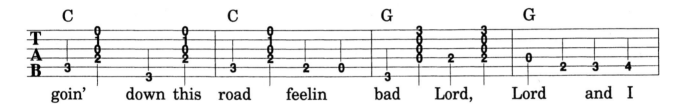

goin' down this road feelin bad Lord, Lord and I

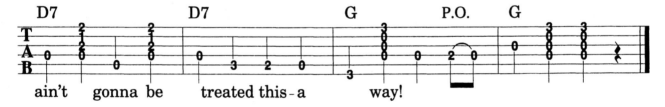

ain't gonna be treated this-a way!

Verse

1. I'm going where the weather suits my clothes.
   I'm going where them chilly winds never blow.
   I'm going where the climate suits my clothes Lord,
   Lord and I ain't gonna be treated this-a way.
   Chorus

2. These two dollar shoes they hurt my feet.
   These two dollar shoes they hurt my feet.
   These two dollar shoes they hurt my feet Lord, Lord
   and I ain't gonna be treated this-a way.
   Chorus

3. They raised me on cornbread and beans.
   The jailer wouldn't gimme enough to eat.
   They raised me on cornbread and beans Lord, Lord
   and I ain't gonna be treated this-a way
   Chorus

Turkey In The Straw

Traditional
Key of G

Starting Pitch

Verse

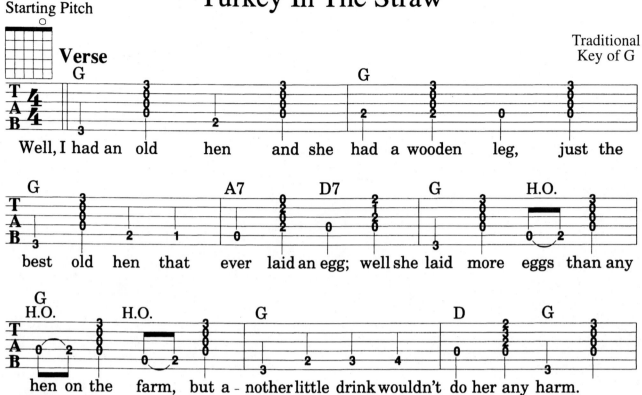

Well, I had an old hen and she had a wooden leg, just the

best old hen that ever laid an egg; well she laid more eggs than any

hen on the farm, but a - nother little drink wouldn't do her any harm.

Chorus

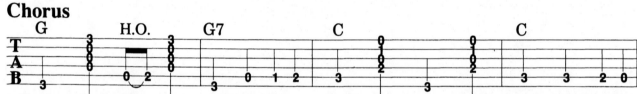

Turkey in the hay, in the hay, hay hay! Turkey in the straw, in the straw, straw straw

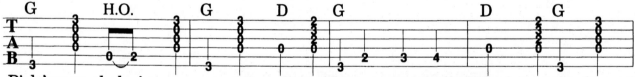

Pick 'em up, shake 'em up, any way at all, and hit up a tune called "Turkey in the Straw"

Well, I hitched up the wagon
and I drove down the road,
With a two horse wagon and a four horse load;
Well I cracked my whip and the lead horse sprung,
And I said "Goodbye" to the wagon tonged.
Chorus

Well, if frogs had wings and snakes had hair
And automobiles went a-flying thro'the air;
Well if watermelons grew
on a huckleberry vine,
We'd have winter in the summer time.
Chorus

Oh, I went out to milk
and I didn't know how,
I milked a goat instead of a cow.
A monkey sitting on a pile of straw,
A-winkin' his eyes at his mother-in-law.
Chorus

Well, I come to the river but I couldn't get across,
So I paid five dollars for an old blind horse,
Well, he wouldn't go ahead
and he wouldn't stand still,
So he went up and down like an old saw mill.
Chorus

Red Haired Boy

Traditional
Key of G
Capo on the 2nd Fret

Starting Pitch

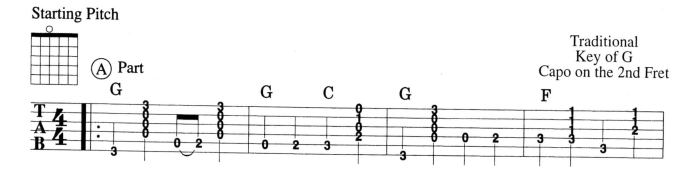

(A) Part

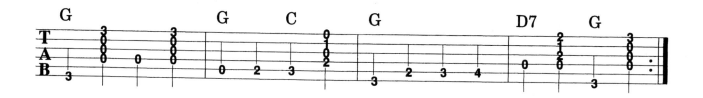

(B) Part

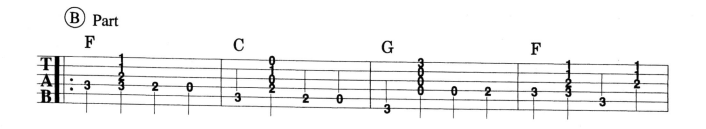

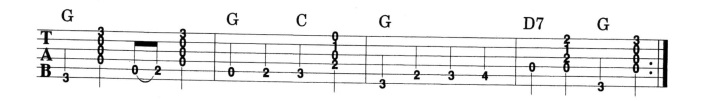

Freight Train

I like to use "Freight Train" in my teaching because it is crammed full of hammer-ons. Also, the chord structure is different than the standard three-chord progressions found in most bluegrass songs. This song was written by Elizabeth Cotten. It fits most of the traditional bluegrass criteria. It's a song about pain and suffering, death and dying. The element that has always fascinated me was that Miss Cotten was 13 years old when she wrote it.

Starting Pitch

Traditional
Key of C

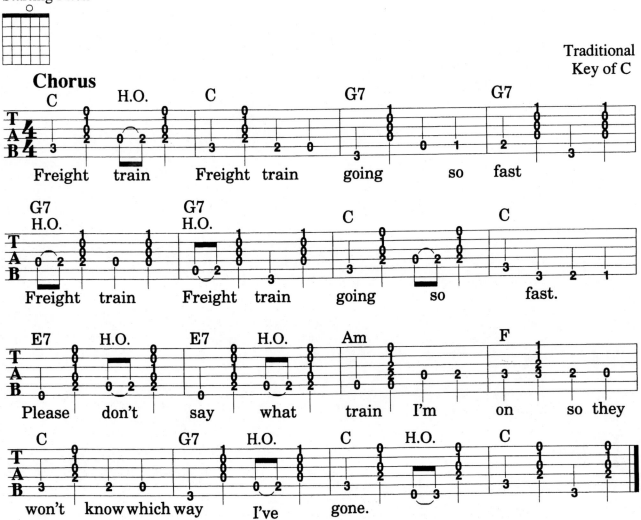

The Verses

1. When I'm dead and in my grave,
   No more good times will I crave,
   Place the stones at my head and feet
   And tell them all that I've gone to sleep.
   Chorus

2. When I die, Lord, bury me deep,
   Way down on old Chestnut Street,
   So I can hear old Number Nine
   As she comes rolling by.
   Chorus

3. When I die, Lord, bury me deep,
   Way down on old Chestnut Street,
   Place the stones at my head and feet
   And tell them all I've gone to sleep.
   Chorus

My Home's Across The Blueridge Mountains

Here is another great tune written out in the key of C. This is a two-chord song. It uses just the C and G7. There are many walks from one chord to another. By now you are a master of the bass walks, hammer-ons and pull-offs. You may not be as accomplished and proficient with the faster down-up runs. The first run of this nature that we will learn is in the third measure. It is used as a C-to-C run. Practice this run by itself by playing the measure over and over. After about 20 times through, you should start to smooth out a little. The speed will come later. After you learn this run, try to place it into other songs that have C-to-C measures. Be sure to follow the arrows indicating the down-up's. This is the only way that this run, or any other eighth-note runs, will smooth out and get fast.

Starting Pitch

Traditional
Key of C

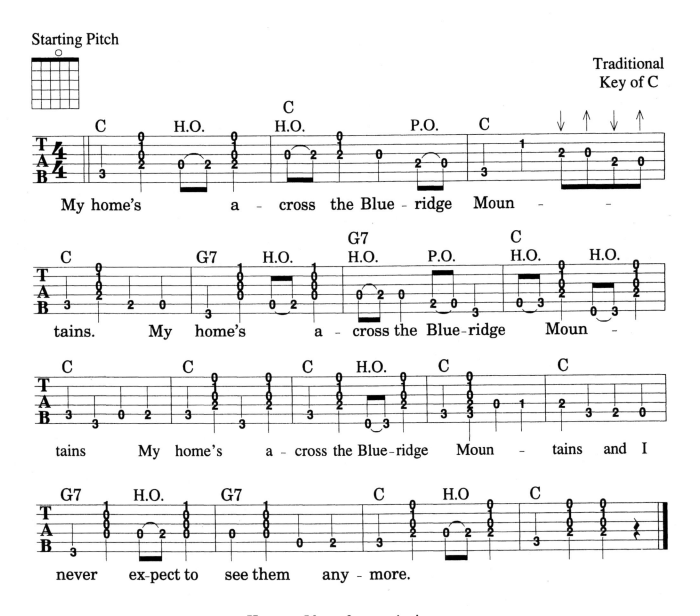

How can I keep from crying!
How can I keep from crying!
How can I keep from crying when I
Never expect to see you anymore?

Hand Me Down My Walking Cane

This tune is written out in the back-up style of Norman Blake. Norman is not only one of my heroes, but I'm proud to say he's also a friend. Norman has one of the smoothest right hands in the flatpicking world today (see the section in my Mel Bay book *The Complete Flatpicking Guitar Book* entitled "The Flatpickers That Influence The Flatpickers" for more on Norman Blake).

Besides having bass-walk runs all over the place, we will also be working on three new runs. The first run is in measure 7. It is used as a G-to-G run. First, you will be walking from D7 to G. Hold the G chord when you finish the D7 run. Hit the 6th string, then strum. Remove your finger from the 5th string and hit the 5th string open (down), then hit the 2nd fret (up). Go to the 4th string and go through the same motions.

Next we will look at measure 11. This is another G-to-G run. Again, start on the 6th string, then strum. After you strum, remove your fingers and hit the next three notes on the 5th string (down-up-down), cross your pick over the 4th string, and swing up. This up-swing on the 4th string is very important. Many of my students, when first learning this type of run, often hit the run going down-up-down-down. They say that since they are going down anyway, why can't they just hit the last note down? There are several reasons. The most important is that by hitting two fast eighth notes down you will be out of time—you end up being either early or late. Your right hand is supposed to be in time just like a metronome. You've seen them going back and forth, but you've never seen them click on the same side twice. It can't be done. If your right hand is to emulate a metronome, then you will have to go down-up on all eighth notes.

Measure 12 is the last measure that may give you trouble. The difficulty lies in the down-up run of eighth notes. Keep in mind that the last four notes in this measure equal the same amount of time as the first two. It should take only two beats to hit all four eighth notes. Good luck!

Starting Pitch

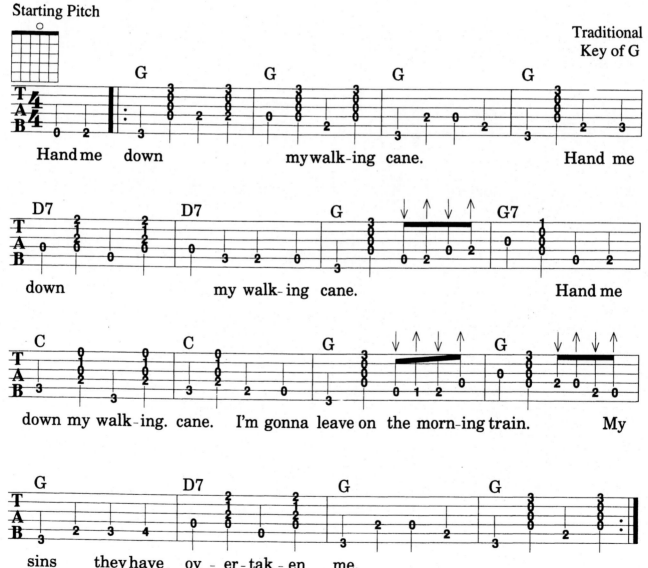

2. Hand me down that bottle of corn.
Hand me down that bottle of corn.
Hand me down that bottle of corn.
I'm gonna get drunk just a sure as I'm born
My sins they have overtaken me.

3. I got drunk and I got in jail.
I got drunk and I got in jail.
I got drunk and I got in jail aint
got no money for to go my bail.
My sins they have overtake me.

4. The beans was tough and the meat was fat.
The beans was tough and the meat was fat.
The beans was tough and the meat was fat.
Oh good God I couldn't eat that.
My sins they have overtaken me.

5. If I die in Tennessee.
If I die in Tennessee.
If I die in Tennessee then
ship me back C.O.D.
My sins they have overtaken me.

(L) Beppe Gambetta, Steve, Stephen Bennet, (R) Slavik Hanslik At a Flatpicking workshop in Winfield, Kansas 1992 we were in Flatpicking Heaven!

Momma Don't Allow No

This is our last installment in the rhythm section. We have bass walks, hammer-ons, pull-offs and eighth-note runs. You shouldn't need much instruction with this tune. The only place I want to point out is in the 3rd and 15th measures. This is the Lester Flatt G run. Be sure to follow the arrows and watch your speed. Keep the tempo steady. You shouldn't slow down in order to hit the eighth-note measures. If you need to slow down to play these measures, then you will have to play the hard parts by themselves until they are the same speed as the rest of the song.

For more information on bass-walk runs and rhythm, check out my Mel Bay book *The Complete Flatpicking Guitar Book.* Take your time learning these songs, and practice with the recording that accompanies this book.

Let's Work On Picking the Lead
Find the Notes On the Guitar

You already know how to read the tablature. Let's go on to some basic theory.

A B C D E F G

This is as hard as it gets. Not really, but you felt really good for a few seconds, now didn't you? You have to remember that the notes are arranged alphabetically A through G, and after G it starts all over again with A and goes through to G, and around this circle forever. Between some of these notes are sharps/flats. *There are two places that do not have sharps/flats between them. They are B-C and E-F.* There is no B♯ or E♯. So your notes will be in alphabetical order with sharps between all of them, except whenever you get to a B note, the next note will be C, and whenever you get to an E note, the next note will be F. Another way to look at this concept is to picture a piano keyboard. You have black and white keys. In fact, the keys alternate between black and white except for two places. They are the B and C keys (no black key between them) and the E and F notes (no black key between them).

Let's practice something. With your guitar in the normal position on your knee—hit the first string. This note is an E. Now push the first fret. This note is an F. Remember that there are no sharps between the E and the F note, meaning that there are no frets between the notes. Now hit the 2nd fret. This is an F♯ note. The next fret is a G, then G♯, A, A♯, B, etc. What comes after B? Remember that **there are no sharps between B and C**. What we have just done is to run your notes on the first string up to the 7th fret. You need to be able to run your notes all the way up to the 12th fret. When you make it up to the 12th fret, calling the names of the fretted notes out loud all the way, you should be one full octave up from where you started. This means that the name of the open string will be the same as the 12th-fret note. If this occurs, you have run your notes successfully.

If you have never read notes before, don't give up trying. You can learn to read your notes in just a few days. You already understand how to read the tablature, so use the tab as a reference to the notes. In an attempt to ease your mind a little, there are only a few instances where the notes will be higher than the 4th fret with the exception of the 1st string. So if the note is a high G, normally found on ht 1st string, and you find it on the chart on the 2nd string—8th fret, well, I probably didn't mean it to be on the 2nd string. Use the tab at this point to cross-reference the location of the note. After you go through a few of these songs by using the notes, you will get the hang of the system. It's not too hard unless you think it is.

Finding The Notes On The Guitar

44

Jenny Linde Polka

This is a good tune to start off with. All of the quarter notes (like in the first measure) are hit with a down swing, and the eighth notes (like the two notes tied together in the second measure) are hit down then up. Both tied notes take the same amount of time to hit as a regular quarter note. Keep the tempo steady, and play along with the tape.

The first eight measures are the actual melody of the song. Be sure to use the fingerings as they are marked. It will make this arrangement a little easier.

Measure 9 begins a variation section. Watch out for the down-ups. The 8 eighth notes in measure 9 should (we hope) take the same amount of time as the 1st measure to complete.

Measure 17 begins the (B) part, which is the chorus. Measure 18 should be fingered as it is marked. One word about this measure is to hold all the notes from the beginning of the measure. This will give you m ore sustain and let the notes ring out longer.

Watch out for the arrow marks!

Traditional
Arr. by Steve Kaufman

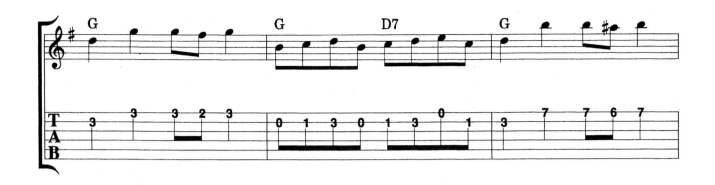

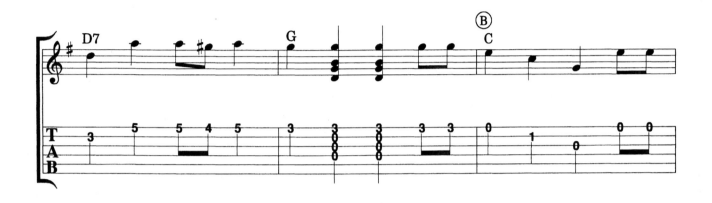

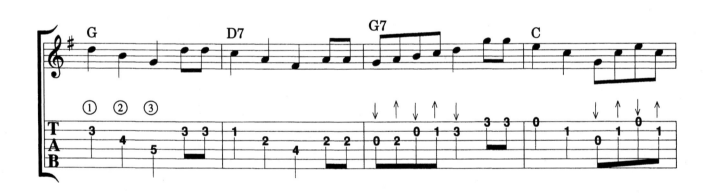

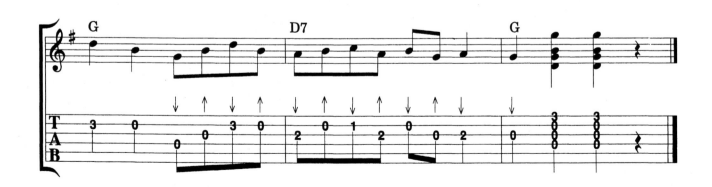

Momma Don't Allow No "Guitar Pickin' Round Here"

This is a classic "jam" tune. It is based on a standard bluegrass chord structure. This solo is pretty straight-forward with only a few places to watch out for.

Measure 2 is somewhat tricky. You have to follow the arrows.

The next measure to watch out for is measure 7. The fingering is the tricky part with this one. Have fun with it.

Traditional
Arr. by Steve Kaufman

Freight Train

With Hammer-Ons

Remember how to perform a hammer-on? The attack of the left-hand fingers is the key to a loud, crisp, clear hammer-on. It doesn't have to be a very fast movement, but when the finger decides to hammer-on, it has to land on the fingerboard with a vengeance.

This version of "Freight Train" is played mostly out of the chords. Hold the chord that is written above the measure that you are working on. The melody notes are found either in the chord that you are holding or within a fret of what you are holding. Be sure to hold the chords. It will make this arrangement a lot easier. The C run at the end of the piece is a little tricky. Watch out for the arrow markings, and play the hammer-ons with clarity.

Elizabeth Cotten
Arr. by Steve Kaufman

50

Freight Train
Pull-Offs, Hammer-Ons and Runs

Now we have a slightly more complex version of "Freight Train." We still have a lot of hammer-ons, but now we are putting in some pull-offs and some interchangeable runs. They are interchangeable because you can now see how they fit into this song in order to create movement from one measure, or chord, to another.

Measure 6 needs mention because many of my students get hung up on this kind of run. Be sure to follow the arrows and cross over the higher string and swing up. Don't stop here. Go to the next measure and keep the down-ups coming.

Measure 13 is the start of a great C-to-G7-and-back-to-C run. As you go through this book, and some of my others, see if you can find other songs that have a C-to-G7-and-back-to-C situation that this run can slip into. This is the basis of improvising. More on that later.

Traditional
Arr. by Steve Kaufman

Way Faring Stranger

This song is a lot like "Freight Train." It is based on playing the melody "out of the chords." This arrangement is loaded with hammer-ons and pull-offs and interconnecting runs.

Some of the more difficult spots are in the handling of the minor chords. For many of you, these are new. It will take a while to get used to holding these minor chords, but think back on how difficult a G chord was when you first learned it and how quickly you became accustomed to it.

The first part (verse) is 16 measures long, with measure 17 starting the chorus. For the most part throughout this section, hold down the chord above the measure for ease in playing the song.

Measure 23 has a bend in it. Whenever you bend a note, you are to use two or three fingers. This measure has a 3rd-fret bend note in it. Place your 1st finger on the 2nd fret and your 2nd finger on the 3rd fret. Pull both fingers at the same time and try to make them touch the 4th string. This is the bend. You want to use several fingers because it evenly distributes all of the pressure needed to bend a note. That about wraps up my part of this tune. Get on it and have fun.

Traditional
Arr. by Steve Kaufman

52

53

My Home's Across The Blueridge Mountains

This tune is written with the main melody part first and a variation on the melody second. The variation is going to be our introduction to crosspicking. The first 16 measures should pose no problem. Be sure to take your time. Have all of the fundamentals under your belt before spending your time on the crosspicking section. Crosspicking, by definition, is hitting three consecutive strings and then starting the pattern over. In order to start the pattern the second time you must cross over the middle of the three strings. This is where the term "crosspicking" came from. It is an ancient art handed down through the generations, and it is a standard part of bluegrass flatpicking.

Measure 5 of the variational page is where I want to direct your attention first. This is the first measure that I want you to practice. It is all open strings, so your left hand doesn't have to worry about doing anything. Just play the open notes in a down-up fashion. Be sure that when you hit the 4th string for the first time it is a down swing, the second time in this measure it is an up swing, and the last time is a down. Then you can be pretty sure that you have crosspicked this measure correctly. Play all of the notes steadily. Put a repeat sign around this measure (in your mind) and play it hundreds of times. I tell my students to play a practice measure until someone throws something at them. After you get this measure down, you can go on to the rest of the piece. Have fun with the crosspicking.

Traditional
Arr. by Steve Kaufman

My Home's Across The Blueridge Mountains
Crosspicking

Traditional
Arr.by Steve Kaufman

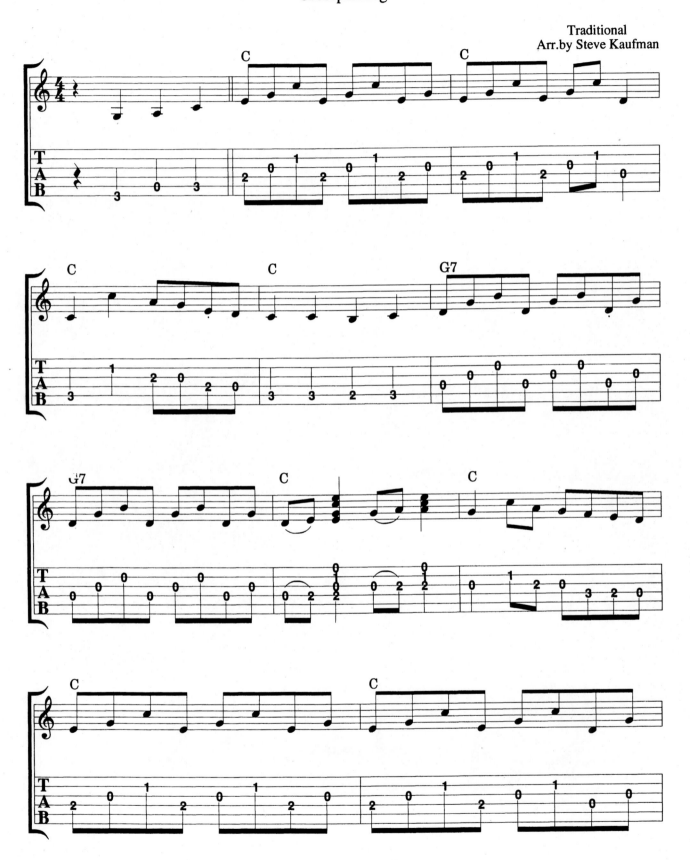

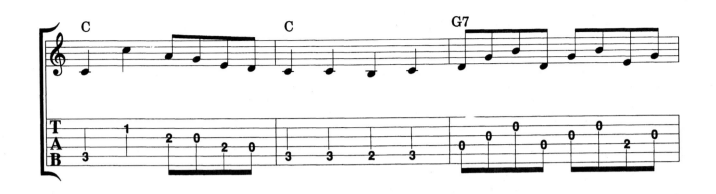

57

Turkey In The Straw

This is our first fiddle tune that we are going to learn how to pick. Fiddle tunes are a big part of learning how to flatpick. They are almost always instrumentals. They generally have more notes per second that vocals do, and they incorporate scale work in such a way that the picker doesn't realize he or she is playing scales. Fiddle tunes usually have two parts, called "A" and "B." If there was a third part it would be called the "C" part. This has nothing to do with the chords in the song.

This tune has repeat signs at the very beginning, telling you that there are repeat signs somewhere else. The second set of repeat signs are at the end of the eighth measure. You go back to the repeat signs at the beginning when you get to this point. Over this measure is a bracket with a "1" in it, and the next measure has a bracketed "2" in it. These are your first and second endings. Play from the top. Go through the first ending to the repeat sign. Go back to the top and play down to the bracketed 1st ending. Skip over this ending and go on to the second ending. Now play the (B) part. It has a repeat sign without the 1st and 2nd endings. This means that you must simply play this part twice. Be sure to practice your chords as many times as you practice the lead melody.

The hardest parts in this version are the eighth notes in the 3rd, 7th, and 16th measures. Be sure to follow the down-ups and you'll get through it fine.

Traditional
Arr. by Steve Kaufman

The Wreck Of The Old Ninety Seven

    I have grouped the next two tunes together because of their chord/lead design. Both arrangements are melodic and rhythmic in the sense that in most of the measures you will hit the melody note and follow it with a strum.

    "Wreck of the Old '97" has a few tricky measures that I would like to go over with you. After you hit the 3 pick-up notes at the beginning, you are to hold your C chord. Doing this will make the 1st measure all right-handed. Measure two is played from within the C chord. Perform the pull-off, and hammer-on while you leave your first and third finger in the C-chord position. You only need to move and remove the 2nd finger. Measure 10 is played the same way.

Traditional
Arr. By Steve Kaufman

59

Home, Sweet Home

"Home, Sweet Home" has many of the same techniques that were found in "Old '97." The melody is different. We have more hammer-ons, and the tune is longer but the fundamentals are the same. Try to hold the chord that is written over the measure while you play through each measure. It makes a world of difference by way of sustaining the notes and easing up the left-hand fingerings. I try to get my students to think, look and plan ahead. I tell them to set up what they are playing. Ease in playing is in the set-up. Hold the chords or groups of notes down whenever possible.

Measure 15 is a good example of an interchangeable run. It is a C run that ends on C. It can replace any measure that starts and ends as this one does. An instance of this is the 15th measure of the "B" part. It is almost the same exact run, but there is a slight variance in the eighth notes. Swap these two runs out and listen for the way you like it best. Always be on the lookout for interchangeable runs and learn to switch them in other songs.

A more complete listening version of "Home, Sweet Home" can be found on my "To the Lady" recording.

Traditional
Arr. by Steve Kaufman

Cripple Creek

"Cripple Creek" is written in the key of A. In most instances, the key of A will mean the second position. This procedure is accomplished by using your first finger for all of the second-fret notes, the second finger for all of the third-fret notes, the third finger for the fourth-fret and the little finger for the fifth-fret notes. Since there are no first-fret notes in this arrangement, we can stay hovering in second position.

"Cripple Creek" is a very fast tune. It is also only four measures long for the first part and four for the second. Each part repeats. I have written this tune with the "A" part and then the "A" part variation. The same format with the second part. It's such a short piece that this was the only way to lengthen it.

The only sites to watch for are the hammer-ons and the eighth-note passages. You should have them down pretty well by now. Good luck with it and have fun. Oh, by the way, this tune when played at full speed is supposed to be over in 15 seconds. That's 7 1/2 seconds for the "A" part with the variation. The same for the "B" part. Look at this as less than 1 second per measure. If you can play "Cripple Creek" at this speed, then you should not fear any parking-lot jam. Start slow and work your way up. *If you can't play it slow...you won't be able to play it fast.*

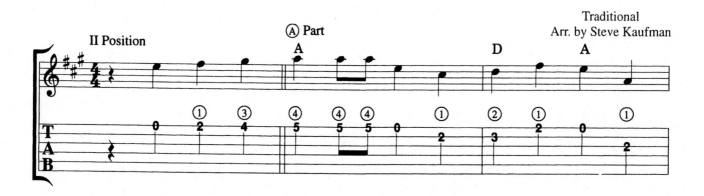

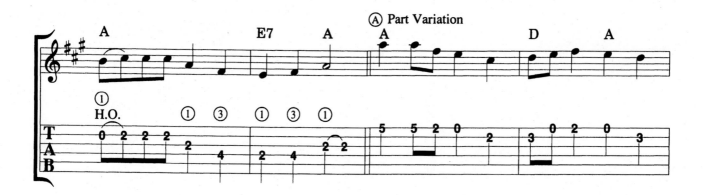

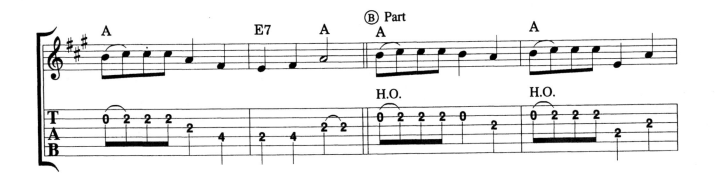

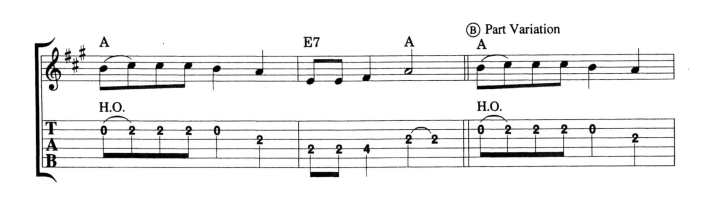

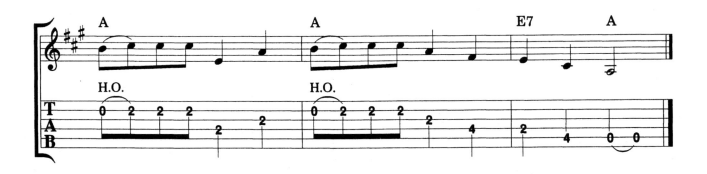

The Girl I Left Behind

I first heard this tune on a Red Rector (mandolin) and Norman Blake (guitar) duet album (actually, I first heard this tune at the end of a Bugs Bunny cartoon). It's an old Civil War tune as the words in the rhythm section will clue you in on.

As you can see, hear and tell, the tunes are starting to get more difficult. This tune is arranged with lots of runs. The measures to look out for are: 2, 6, 15 and 16. The first three mentioned are difficult, but they are all the same. Be sure to use the fingerings that are marked. Use the 1st ending and repeat. Then skip the 1st ending, going on to the 2nd ending. Go through the "B" part and use your 1st and 2nd endings the same way.

Watch out for the down-ups!

Remember—play the chords as many times as you play the lead.

Traditional
Arr. by Steve Kaufman

64

Home, Sweet Home
Crosspicking

Those of you that have been to my workshops or seen my stage shows know that I love crosspicking. If you are a solo performer, or like playing ballads, you need to work on crosspicking and have it as fluid as breathing. It takes a quarter of a lifetime, so you had better get started. It really only takes a few months and you can be crosspicking like the professionals.

Crosspicking takes the melody notes and wraps them into and around a roll pattern of some kind. It's like fingerpicking the melody within a roll pattern. Work on this variation of "Home, Sweet Home" only after you have learned the first version so that you will be aware which notes are the melody and which notes are the roll, filler-pattern notes.

Start measure 1 with a first-and-second-finger C chord. Follow the arrows and keep the timing steady. This measure is the basic crosspicking example of all of the crosspicking measures. Keep in mind that the measures have 8 eighth notes in them, tied together in groups of four. "1+2+3+4" is the way to count each note. The down swings are on the numbers and the up swings are on the "+." This equals two sets of eighth notes. The point of this roaming lecture is most of the time the 2 sets of 4 eighth notes end up as 2 sets of threes plus a little extra. It ends up sounding like da-da-da, rest, da-da-da, rest, da-da. You want it to sound like da-da-da-da-da-da-da-da. Just like the hum of a sewing machine.

The biggest trouble spot in this arrangement will be the fourth eighth note. It should be an up swing, and most beginning crosspickers make it a down swing, throwing off the rhythm.

The entire first part is a forward roll pattern. The first and part of the second measure of the "B" part are a backwards roll pattern. No need for concern, just practice. This tune ought to keep you busy for a little while. Not much more to say about this tune—just watch out for the timing and your down-up swings. Have fun!

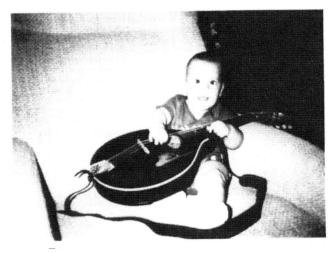

Mark picking the mandolin at the age of 4 months—maybe the next National Champion.
Watch out—Mr. Grisman!

Home, Sweet Home

Crosspicking

Traditional
Arr. by Steve Kaufman

Red Haired Boy
Little Beggar Man

"Red Haired Boy" has two names. The other name is "Little Beggar Man." Both of them are identical and played in the key of A. We are going to learn this one in the key of G and capo up to the second fret. This will put us in the key of A.

You shouldn't have too much trouble playing through this one. The harder measures are typically the ones with the eighth notes in them. Be careful and pay attention to the right-hand motion. *Remember that the down-ups dictate whether the timing is correct.*

I think that the hardest single measure in this arrangement will be the second measure. You have to be sure to swing up on the 2nd string open (at the end of the eighth-note phrase). Most people don't (at first), and they get out of time. This same measure is repeated several times throughout this arrangement—beware.

Play through the first part using the 1st ending, then repeat the first part. The second time through *be sure to use the 2nd ending.* Then go on to the "B" part. You should notice several similarities between the last few measures of each part. The "B" section has been written out with no repeats. Instead, I have written a "B" part variation. This variation takes the place of the repeated section. You are still playing this part twice, just not the same way.

69

Arkansas Traveler
The Bare Melody

This song is written out two ways. The first version is what I would consider the straight melody. You must always learn the "bare bones" melody of a song before any variations. The reason is that variations stray from the melody, and the more complex the variation, the farther you go from the melody. You have to know what tune you are varying in the first place in order to understand the other versions. This is also written out in the key of D. There are not going to be any first-fret notes in this arrangement, so place your fingers in second position. Your first finger will hit all of the 2nd frets, and your little finger will hit all of the 5th frets. Your 2nd and 3rd fingers will hit the frets in between. Be sure to use the little finger on the 5th frets. Many of my students get lazy and try to slip the 3rd finger to the 5th fret, but I tell them the only reason to do this would be if they lost their 4th finger. Don't be lazy.

Watch out in measure 4. The arrows should guide you. Be sure to use the repeats.

Traditional
Arr. by Steve Kaufman

70

Arkansas Traveler

Now that you have mastered the first version of "Arkansas Traveler," it's time to go on to a variation. This arrangement is written out with a high 1st part and then, instead of repeating the same section, we are going to the next lower octave. We won't be playing it exactly the same way an octave lower, but it'll be close.

You should also play this one out of 2nd position. There is only one first-fret note in this arrangement, and you shouldn't need any particular guidance when you get to that measure.

Measure 8 has a hammer-on from the 3rd to 4th fret. Use the 2nd and 3rd fingers. Do not slide—hammer it on.

The "B" part is written similarly to the "A" part. We start with the melody in one register and then drop it down an octave to play the variation. This is a typical method of playing and arranging a tune. You should start to play songs that you already know and try to move them up or down an octave. You already know how the runs sound, so when you shift them up or down you will learn the runs in a different location. I remember that when I first started working on my own arrangements I would shift runs up or down in the same key. It's a great practice exercise if nothing else.

The 3rd measure of the "B" part may have a new chord for you. It's called a D♯ diminished, represented by the small "o." This is a great chord that dictates a chordal movement of some kind. When you listen other songs, listen for this chord. It is used a lot in Texas-style rhythm.

Good luck with this version of "Arkansas Traveler," and be sure to pay attention to the right hand. You'll need it on this one.

Traditional
Arr. by Steve Kaufman

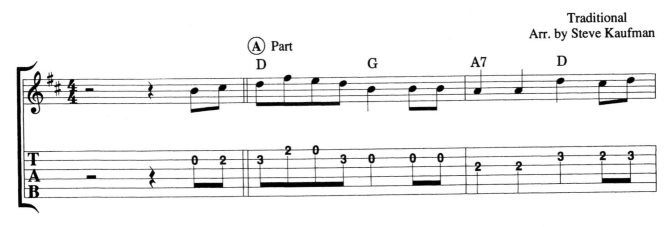

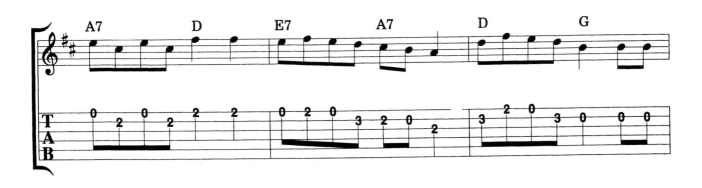

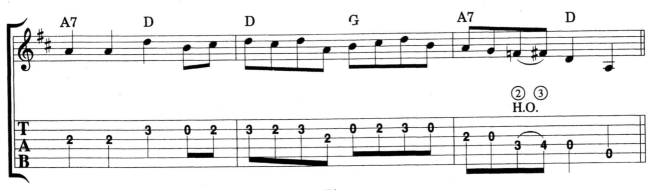

Ⓑ Part Variation

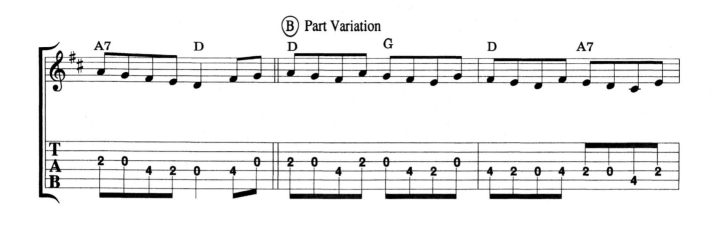

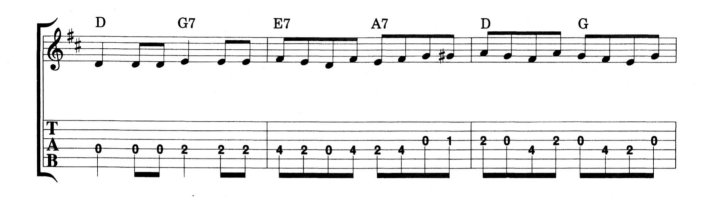

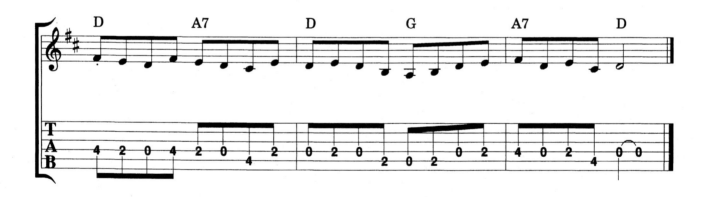

73

Cripple Creek
A Little Fancier

This second version of "Cripple Creek" is a lot of fun to play. It's more in a "Texas style" of flatpicking. The melody notes are interwoven into connecting runs. You can always hear the melody in this and most of my other arrangements. This is very important to consider whenever you are making up your own arrangements to songs. Don't just stick a run of notes together without first envisioning the final melodic substance of the piece. In other words, don't just play a bunch of "junk" licks that have no socially significant value.

Measures 1 through 7 are completely closed runs. This means that because there are no open strings, the passage can be moved to any position on the fingerboard, thus changing the key in which you are playing. If you moved the first measure up 2 frets, you would be playing in the key of B, and so on.

Be sure to use the correct fingerings. They will prove very helpful.

Measure 3 has a slide into the 5th and 6th frets using the 1st and 2nd fingers. Just slide from one fret before the 5th and 6th frets. This same passage comes up several more times in this arrangement and is played the same each time.

The last 4 measures make up a great A run. It lasts for 4 measures and can be chopped off at any point. Be on the look-out for runs that can fit into other songs.

Good luck with this one.

Traditional
Arr. by Steve Kaufman

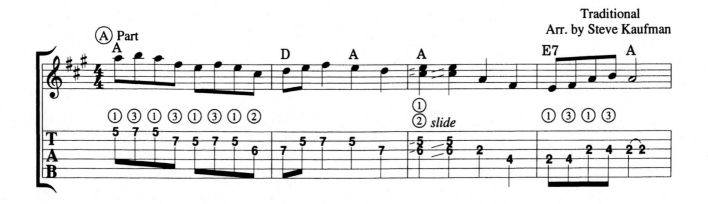

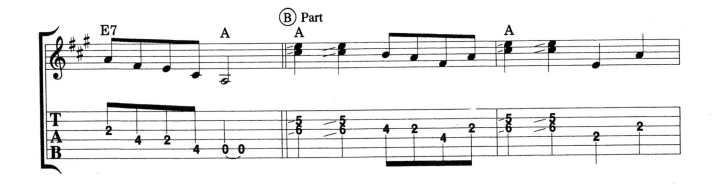

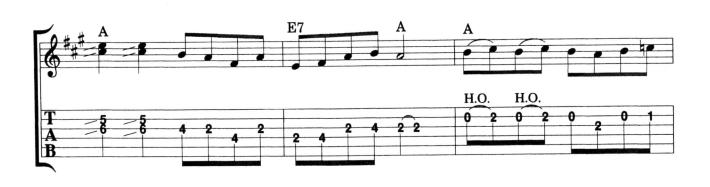

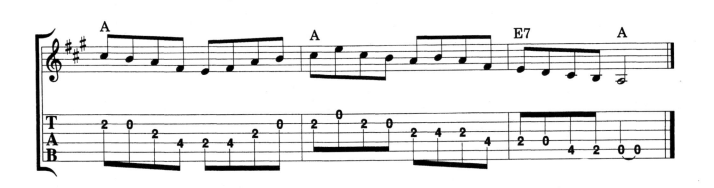

Turkey In The Straw

A Little Harder

I like to teach this tune for many reasons: 1) you get a chance to play longer runs than the other songs that we have covered so far; 2) it works out your 1st and 3rd fingers as they pummel the 2nd and 4th frets; 3) you get a chance to hit tied eighth notes. Whenever you come across tied eighth notes, they will probably cause you to hit either 2 downs in a row or 2 ups in a row. An example of this is measure 7. You are to hit two ups in a row. The best way I have found to guarantee correct timing through these types of measures is to hit all of the notes (down-up) and get used to the timing. Then leave out the note that is tied by faking the swing. This fake of the swing will put a block of time, or a gap, where it should be. Swing down-up, fake the down, then swing up.

The end of the 2nd ending is tricky. You are to hit the last 2 eighth notes and then slide into the "B" part. Hit the open 3rd string down, then come up on the A note (2), slide. Then come up on the D note (3), fake the down swing and come up on the B. Three up swings in a row.

There are many tied eighth notes in this song, and they all have to be hit correctly in order to sound like the "Turkey In the Straw" that we are all used to. Be careful, take your time, and have fun with it.

Traditional
Arr. by Steve Kaufman

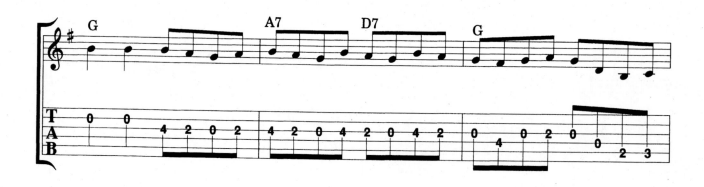

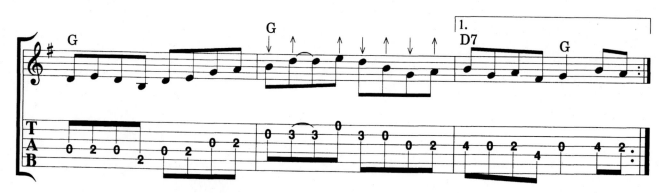

76

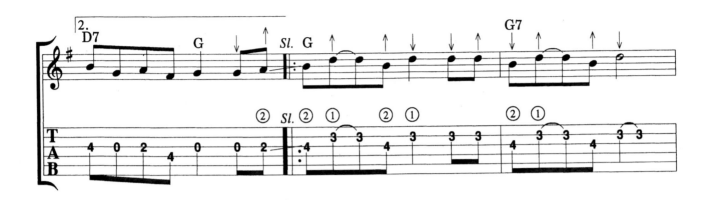

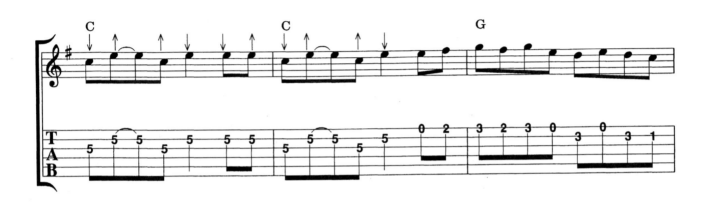

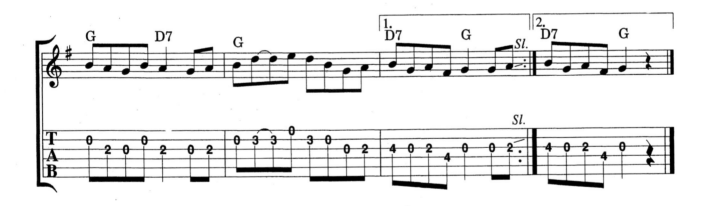

To hear more "Turkey In the Straw," listen to Steve's "Breaking Out" recording.

Momma Don't Allow No "Flat Top" Picking Round Here

We have reached the final tune in the book. By now you have been well acquainted with hammer-ons, pull-offs, slides, double-note slides, rhythm, bass walks, 3/4 time, 4/4 time ballads, fiddle tunes and traditional vocal songs. After typing that list out, I've come to realize that you have learned a lot. If any section of the preceding list is a little shaky or unsure, then I suggest you go back over it. You may remember that the point of this book is "You Can Teach Yourself To Flatpick."

Almost all of the above elements are found in this last tune. It is a great jamming tune where all of the instruments get a chance to shine. The vocalist calls out the instrument that Momma don't 'low around here, and whoever that is, is the next one to pick.

The first real tricky spot is in measure 2. You have a pull-off between two sets of eighth notes. Be sure to dig your finger under the string when you perform the pull-off. This will insure a crisp-sounding pull-off. Hit only the first note of the pull-off and let your left hand sound the second note. Play 2 up swings in a row. Measure 7 has a similar pull-off. The notes are different, but the right-hand pull-off is the same.

Measure 11 is a great C run with a hammer-on and a pull-off in the same string of eighth notes. Watch the down-ups here.

Traditional
Arr. by Steve Kaufman

Practice Techniques To Remember

1)   Always place your left-hand fingertips as close to the next fret as possible without going over the next fret. This will guarantee a note free of buzzes and rattles. It will also take the least amount of finger pressure to fret the note.

2)   Practice playing very slowly and strongly. This will help develop power, volume, clarity, and tone. If you can't play a song slowly, then you won't be able to play it quickly.

3)   Practice playing very quickly (in the privacy of your own home). This will help to develop speed and accuracy. You must realize before you attempt this speed practice that you will probably crash. You must get your fingers used to playing quickly or they will never learn how to play quickly. Don't worry about making mistakes when you practice this technique. It's just used for training.

4)   When you are playing with other musicians and singers, use your ears. Listen to and watch the others. They will telegraph signals to you. Are you playing too loudly or quietly? Are you speeding up the song or dragging it down? Watch the others—they will let you know.

5)   When you are playing with others for the first time, play in the background. Do not attract a lot of attention to yourself unless you are asked to do so. You will have a better chance of being asked back.

6)   Don't get too frustrated or disgusted or mad at yourself. You are attempting a hobby in which perfection is rare. Everybody makes mistakes. This is true in almost every field or walk in life. The professionals hide their mistakes, whereas the beginner doesn't yet know how to hide them. Everybody makes them. I learned a long time ago just to smile at the mistakes and try to make the best of it.

Remember this always—you are doing this for fun, so have fun with it and grow into the best guitarist that you can be! I wish you all the best, and feel free to write to me care of Mel Bay Publications or call my 1-800-FLATPIK number with any questions that you may have and I'll try to answer them all.

Best always,
Steve Kaufman
Steve Kaufman

The Equipment Steve Used In This Series

Taylor 810 Custom Cutaway Guitar for the lead picking
Gallagher 7-String Cutaway Guitar for the rhythm playing in section 4
Mini Flex internal condenser microphone installed in the Taylor guitar
Shure SM81 Microphone for the Gallagher guitar
Yellow Tortex Medium Gauge Picks—Standard Fender Shape
Dr. Strings--Rare Phosphor Bronze Heavy-medium .13-.56 guage
Schubb Capo's

Photo Credits

The photographs of Steve's guitars, Steve's hands holding the chords, arms and hand positions, Steve's "Breaking Out" and Multi-Instrumental promotional photographs were taken by Tim Everett.

Mark Oliver Dixon Kaufman sleeping in the guitar case at Wilkesboro, N.C. photograph taken by Laura Hicks.

Mark Oliver Dixon Kaufman photo "Pickin' the Mandolin" by Steve Kaufman.

All other photographs were taken by Ken Reynolds.

Other Credits

You Can Teach Yourself To Flatpick cassette was recorded analog to digital at Sleeping Bear Recordings—Alcoa, TN.

All of the tunes in this book were arranged and adapted by Steve Kaufman.

Steve Kaufman's Discography
For Your Listening Pleasure

The Arkansas Traveler - *Steve's newest flatpicking recording. 18 songs equaling 59 minutes and hot as a firecracker. Special guest Michele Voan singing 2 of the cuts. Steve sings 2 and picks 14 instrumentals.* **Available on CD only.**

To The Lady - *One of the most popular Steve Kaufman recordings. 58 minutes of hot fiddle tunes, ballads, 3 original instrumentals, 6 classic tunes. Lots of fun and great listening.* **Available on CD or long-playing cassette**

Breaking Out - *solo Steve Kaufman pickin'. Whiskey Before Breakfast, Jerusalem Ridge, The I Miss You Waltz, Temptation Rag, Faded Love, Turkey In The Straw and more.* **58 minute CD or 38 minute Cassette**

Star of the County Down - *a HOT duo recording with 1985 National Flatpicking Champ Robin Kessinger. The World Is Waiting For The Sunrise, Cattle In The Cane, Calgary Polka and more.* **Cassette only**

Frost On The Window - *a remixed and remastered 44-minute cassette from 1985 with two new cuts. Six tunes were recorded as they were played in the National Flatpicking Championships. Greensleeves, New Camptown Races, Red Wing, Alabama Jubilee, Grey Eagle, Black and White Rag plus 9 other selections.* **Cassette only**

For Your Instructional Needs

The Championship Flatpicking Guitar Book with a 1-hour cassette- *61 pages of advanced finger-burners. Some of the 16 tunes are: Beaumont Rag, Dill Pickle Rag, Grey Eagle, Sally Goodin and Farewell Blues.* **MB Pub.**

The Complete Flatpicking Guitar Book with a 1-hour cassette- *This book is for the beginner and is designed to take you all the way through the intermediate level to the edge of the advanced plane. 101 pages of tips and time-saving information. There are sections on bass walks, making your own arrangements to instrumentals and vocals, chord voicings, backup rhythm and brings you to the styles of Doc Watson, Norman Blake, Dan Crary, Tony Rice and Steve Kaufman.* **MB Pub.**

Flatpicking The Gospels Book with a 1-hour cassette- *144+ pages of gospel songs intended for the beginner/ intermediate levels. This book teaches you how to play the rhythm, a beginner melody, an intermediate melody and the words to 24 great gospel songs.* **MB Pub.**

Power Flatpicking Book with a 1-hour Cassette - *Learn to play in any key. Learn to play in any position or register. Unlock the mysteries of the bluegrass fingerboard and learn to be a "Power Flatpicker". You can throw away that capo now.* **MB Pub.**

Bluegrass Guitar Solos That Every Parking Lot Picker Should Know Vol. 1 - *6 audio cassettes and a 165-page book of standard bluegrass Guitar Jamming Tunes written in notes and tablature. Learn to play: Ragtime Annie, Big Sandy River, Bill Cheatham, Billy In The Low Ground, Gold Rush, Double Eagle, Flop-Eared Mule, Fisher's Hornpipe, Forked Deer, Blackberry Blossom, Old Joe Clark, Turkey In The Straw, Soldier's Joy, St. Anne's Reel, Nothing To It, Arkansas Traveller, Red-Haired Boy, Sweet Georgia Brown, Salt Creek and Whiskey Before Breakfast.* **Level: Beginner, Intermediate, Advanced H. T. Inc.**

Bluegrass Guitar Solos That Every Parking Lot Picker Should Know Vol. 2 - *A sister series with the same format as Vol. 1. 6 cassettes with 20 more standard tunes for you to learn. You will learn to play: Alabama Jubilee, Black Mountain Rag, Blackberry Rag, Cherokee Shuffle, Cricket On The Hearth, Dixie Hoedown, Down Yonder, Eighth Of January, John Hardy, June Apple, Katie Hill, Liberty, Mississippi Sawyer, Peacock Rag, Red Wing, Stony Creek, Temperance Reel, Texas Gales, Wheel Hoss and, yes, The Wildwood Flower.* **Level: Beginner, Intermediate, Advanced H. T. Inc.**

What To Play When The Singing Stops- Bluegrass Guitar Solos Every Parking Lot Picker Should Know Vol. 3. *This is the same format as Vol. 1 and 2 except this series is designed to teach you to play the solos for 20 of the most standard bluegrass vocals. 115-page book with 6 cassettes.* **Level : Beginner, Intermediate, Advanced H. T. Inc.**

Learning To Flatpick 2- <u>The Video</u>- *A video produced for the beginner and intermediate level. Lots of tips and time-saving remedies to many of the mysteries of guitar picking. Some of the tunes covered in this 90-minute video are The Wildwood Flower, Old Joe Clark and Down Yonder.* **Level: beginner/intermediate. H. T. Inc.**

Learning To Flatpick 3- <u>The Video</u> - *this has been developed for the int./advanced player. Designed to help develop Speed and Style. Many tunes are broken down in this 90 minute video.* **Level: Intermediate/ Advances H.T. Inc.**

Basic Bluegrass Rhythm- <u>The Video</u>- *This 70 minute video is designed to take the beginner to the band ready level of back up guitar. We will cover bass runs, fills, substitution chords and Texas style rhythm.* **Level: Beginner/Intermediate H.T. Inc.**

Easy Gospel Guitar - <u>The Video</u> - *Through this 90-minute video, you will learn to* **play bluegrass/country guitar through your** *favorite gospel songs. Whether you are a beginning or intermediate player, you will* **develop a repertoire** *of tunes and* **add style** *to songs you may already know. Steve slowly plays the accompaniment and melody of each song, then enhances the arrangement with* **basic chords, bass walks, hammer-ons, pull-offs, runs and other techniques.** *You'll soon be playing wonderful arrangements to these well-known tunes: Amazing Grace, Just a Closer Walk With Thee, Old-Time Religion, The Old Rugged Cross, Will The Circle Be Unbroken, What A Friend We Have In Jesus and Cryin' Holy Unto The Lord.* **Level: beg / int. H.T. Inc.**

Steve Kaufman's 2 Hour Bluegrass Work Out - Series 1 and/or Series 2 - *designed as a practice tape this series lets you play along with a band anytime at half speed or full speed. The lead is on the left speaker and the band is on the right speaker. There is very little instruction, the melody's are written in notes in a basic version. This way you can learn the simple melody and then jam with the tape.* **2 -One hour cassettes and book.** *Level : All* **H. T. Inc. Specify Banjo series or all other instruments.**

Steve Kaufman, P.O. Box 1020, Alcoa, TN. 37701 or call 1-800-FLATPIK